JOHN RAMSAY'S CATALOGUE OF
BRITISH DIECAST MODEL TOYS

UPDATING ISSUE TO THE

THIRD EDITION

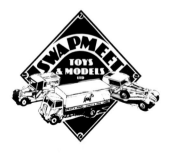

A Swapmeet Toys and Models Ltd Publication
PO Box 21, Bury St. Edmunds, Suffolk, England IP33 2ED

Compiled by John Ramsay

1st Edition published 1984
2nd Edition published 1986
3rd Edition published 1988
Updating Issue to the 3rd Edition published December 1989

ISBN 0 9509319-3-4

Origination by King Design and Advertising Limited, Ipswich

Printing by Fuller Davies Limited, Ipswich

CONTENTS

CORGI TOYS continued

BUDGIE & MORESTONE

EFE — Exclusive First Editions Ltd

SPOT ON MODELS

CRESCENT TOYS

TRIANG MINIC SHIPS

LLEDO 'MODELS OF DAYS GONE'

Abbreviations

Odds and Ends

Advertising in the 4th Edition

Foreword

When the 3rd Edition went to press in June 1988 our next objective was to prepare the 4th Edition and publish it in the Autumn of 1990, thereby maintaining the sequence of a new Edition every two years.

However since the 3rd Edition was published there have been a tremendous number of new issues released by the established manufacturers. In addition with the birth of Exclusive First Editions Ltd, an entirely new and additional range of products have made their debut.

Furthermore considerable price changes have taken place since we last undertook a Market Survey of model prices in the spring of 1988.

Not surprisingly by therefore this Supplement has been prepared with the prime objective of helping collectors keep up to date prior to the next main edition being published late in 1990.

It is therefore to be hoped that by providing full details of the new issues plus information on the 1988/9 price movements we will have assisted collectors bridge the gap between the 3rd and 4th Editions.

The period 1988/9 has been a very busy one for Swapmeet Toys and Models.

Firstly we have formed a long term association with Vectis Models whereby the Catalogue listings will greatly benefit from Roger Mazillius's wide experience and knowledge of the toy collecting market place.

Secondly, we have recently purchased Dr Cecil Gibson's Library and records. Dr. Gibson is probably the doyen of British diecast model collecting having written several books during the sixties including his famous book 'History of British Dinky Toys 1934-1964.' More recently he produced the foreword for Mike and Sue Richardson's superb book 'Dinky Toys and Modelled Miniatures'.

Dr. Gibson's records were compiled during the period 1945 to 1969 and includes his personally recorded details of the model variations issued during this period for all makes of British diecast toys.

It is Dr Gibson's wish that the information in his records is imparted to collectors via the catalogue and this we shall endeavour to do commencing with the 4th Edition.

Finally collectors will notice that the Price and Rarity Grading System employed in the past has been replaced in favour of using one based on quoting a 'Market Price Range'.

From the research we have undertaken, this change will be welcomed by both the trade and collectors alike as one which will provide price guidance on a more realistic and easier to follow basis.

Collectors will appreciate that in an updating Supplement of this type it is not possible to individually review every entry. Nevertheless we have endeavoured to ensure that sufficient price information has been provided to keep collectors fully in the picture of just where the main changes have taken place.

PUBLISHER'S STATEMENT

Accurate birth records do not exist in respect of all the die-cast models issued. Therefore whilst every effort has been made to provide comprehensive information it is inevitable that collectors will have knowledge of models which have not been included. Consequently the compiler will be pleased to receive details of these models in order that they be included in any future editions. Naturally supporting evidence regarding authenticity will be required.

This publication has been prepared solely for use as a reference book and guide to the rarity and asking prices of die-cast model toys.

Whilst every care has been taken in compiling the publication, neither the compiler nor the publishers can accept any responsibility whatsoever for any financial loss which may occur as a result of its use.

MARKET PRICE RANGE GRADING SYSTEM

i)   The price range shown refers to boxed models unless they refer to unboxed prewar or unboxed early post war Dinky Toys as indicated by the text.

ii)   The price gap between the lower and higher figures given indicates the likely price range a collector should expect to pay for a similar model.

iii)   Normally pristine mint boxed models or rarer colours will be priced at the top of the range, with the common colours or the less than pristine models at the lower end.

SELLING MODELS TO THE TRADE

The model value figures produced by the Price Grading System always refer to the likely *asking prices* for models.

They have been prepared solely to give collectors an idea of the amount they might reasonably expect to pay for a particular model.

The figures given are *not* intended to represent the price which will be placed on a model when it is offered for sale to a dealer. This is hardly surprising bearing in mind that the dealer is carrying all the expense of offering a collecting service to his customers which costs money to maintain.

Collectors should therefore not be surprised when selling models to the trade to receive offers which may appear somewhat low in comparison with the figures shown in the catalogue.

Dealers are always keen to replenish their stocks with quality items and will, as a result, normally make perfectly fair and reasonable offers for models. Indeed, depending on the particular models offered to them, the actual offer made may well at times exceed the levels indicated in the catalogue which are only *guidelines* and not firm figures.

One last point when selling models to the trade do get quotations from two or three dealers especially if you have rare models to be sold.

OFFICIAL COMPANY ACKNOWLEDGEMENTS

The name 'MATCHBOX', 'MODELS OF YESTERYEAR', SUPERKINGS' and 'DINKY' are trademarks of the Matchbox Group of companies and are subject to extensive trademark registrations (Marca Registrada) 1987 and 1988.

'CORGI TOYS', 'CORGI CLASSIC', 'CARS OF THE FIFTIES', 'CORGITRONICS' This supplement acknowledges that these trademarks are the property of Corgi Toys Ltd.

'MODELS OF DAYS GONE'
The supplement acknowledges that this trademark is the property of Lledo (London) Ltd.

'BUDGIE TOYS'
The supplement acknowledges that his trademark is the property of Starcourt Ltd.

'E.F.E.' Models
The supplement acknowledges that this trademark is the property of Exclusive First Editions Ltd.

A.   The Chassis Types 1934-1950

1934-38
Criss Cross
Chassis
(CCCH)

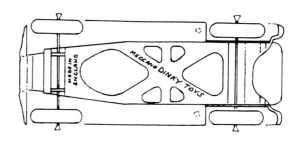

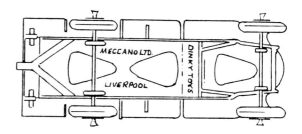

1946-47
Plain
Chassis
(PLCH)

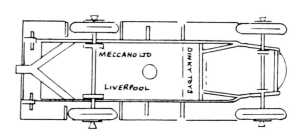

1938-50
Moulded
Chassis
(MCH)

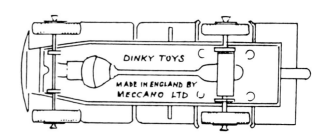

B. The Van Types 1934-1954

28 Series and 280 Series Castings.

1st Type 1934-36	2nd Type 1936-38	3rd Type 1938-54
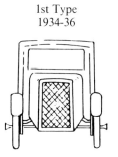		

2 Piece Lead Construction
Metal Wheels
Radiator not cast in.
No Headlights.

Onc Piece Construction
Rubber Tyres (White)
Cast in Radiator
Made of Poor Metal
and liable to disintegrate.

One Piece Construction
Rubber Tyres
Cast in Radiator
Front Bumper
Made of Poor Metal
and liable to disintegrate

C. The Lorry Types 1934-50

25 Series Commercials

1st Type 1934-1938	2nd Type 1938-1940
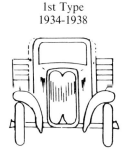	

1st Type No Headlighs on a tinplate Radiator, Open Chassis
2nd Type Headlights on a die-cast Radiator, Open Chassis.

3rd Type 1946-47	4th Type 1947-50

3rd Type This model has the same lorry front as the 2nd Type but has a Plain Chassis.
4th Type Headlights on a die-cast Radiator plus the bumper.

D.   The Heavy Commercial Types 1947-60

1st Type
Foden 1947-52

2nd Type
Foden 1952-55

1st Type
Guy 1947-54

2nd Type
Guy 1954-58

Warrior Type
1959-60

Note the slight difference in the casting around the area of the
number plate between the 1st and 2nd Types of Guy Vehicles.

E.   The Bus Types 1938-63

1st Type
AEC 1938-50

2nd Type
AEC 1950-57

3rd Type
Leyland 1957-63

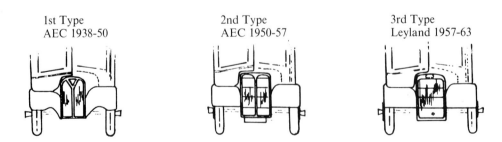

There are three main types although many slight variations in
the castings are thought to exist.
Note the 2nd Type AEC is also referred to as a Guy at times.

Dinky Toys

Review of 3rd Edition Listings

As forecast in the 1988 Market Survey prices for the rarer sets and pristine boxed models have moved strongly ahead in 1988/9.

Indeed world record auction prices were realised for several lots at Phillips of London December 1988 auction. Not surprisingly the marked up asking prices in collectors shops and Toyfairs have reflected thse increased levels.

In addition the prices for both quality unboxed and 'play worn' models have also moved ahead , eg it is now virtually impossible to find a commercial vehicle such as a Foden Flat Truck in any condition for under £25.

Dinky Cars

22 SERIES

22a	Sports Car (Wolseley Hornet)	£300-£500
22b	Sports Coupe (SS Jaguar)	£300-£500

Auction Price Results
22 Series Set
22a Sports Car (red/cream) 22b Sports Coupe (yellow/green) 22c Motor Truck (blue/red) 22d Delivery Van (Orange/blue) 22e Tractor (yellow/green) (G-M)   *Phillips* £2000

23 SERIES

Auction Price Results
23a Racing Car in half dozen trade box 2 red/silver, 4 silver/red (M)   *Phillips* £150
23c Mercedes Racing Cars   5 Models in mint condition in a half dozen trade box, pale blue, dark blue, green, yellow and red (E,M)   *Phillips* £1100

24 SERIES

All issues   £150-£250
Really pristine examples can attract a 50% premium

Auction Price Result
No 24 Set Motor Cars
Early set with grey/red 24a Ambulance in original box 'slight fatigue'   *Phillips* £5000
Later set with cream/red 24a Ambulance in original box 'with fatigue'   *Phillips* £3000

30 SERIES

Pre-war Issues	£150-250
Post War	£70-£100

Auction Price Results
30 set of vehicles in original box and packing 'some fatigue' (30f Ambulance post war not pre war) (E)   *Phillips* £1700
32 Airflow saloon in half dozen Trade Box green, red, maroon, light blue, dark blue, cream (E to M)   *Phillips* £2400

35 SERIES

35a	Saloon Car (Austin Ruby)	£50-£70
35b	Racer add £20 for blue issue	£50-£60

Auction Price Result
35b Racer Five in half dozen trade box (E-M)   *Phillips* £210

36 SERIES

1st	issues (36a,b,c,d,e,f)	£400-£500
2nd	issues (36a,b,c,d,e,f)	£150-£250
3rd	issues (36a,b,c,d,e,f)	£70-£100

Auction Price Result
36b Bentley 3 in half dozen Trade Box (G-E)   *Phillips* £120

38 SERIES

1st	issues (38a,b,c,d)	£100-£150
2nd	issues (38a,b,c,d	£70-£100

Auction Price Result
38e Armstrong Siddeley Coupé in half dozen trade box set of six green with grey interior (M)   *Phillips* £400

39 SERIES

1st	issues (39a,b,c,d,e,f)	£150-£200
2nd	issues (39a,b,c,d,e,f)	£70-£100
	39bu, 39cu, 39eu	£350-£450

Auction Price Results
39a Packard Super 8 tourer green/brown, in half dozen trade box (M)   *Phillips* £300
39d Buick Viceroy saloon 4 maroon, light grey in half dozen Trade Box (E-M)   *Phillips* £380

40 SERIES

All issues 40a-40f   (unboxed) £40-£60
add £40 for correct box
N.B. 40e Standard Vanguard-normal colours are brown and blue. Maroon is scarce and worth double.

Auction Price Results
40b Triumph 1800 half dozen in Trade Box (M)   *Phillips* £320
40g Morris Oxford half dozen in Trade Box (E-M) 4 green, 2 brown   *Phillips* £240

101	Sunbeam Alpine	£80-£100
102	MG Midget	£100-£150
102	MG Midget (green)	£200-£250
103	Austin Healey	£80-£100
104	Aston Martin	£80-£100
105	Triumph TR2	£100-£120
	Yellow body	£150-£200
106	Austin A90 Atlantic	
	Blue/cream	£100-£150
	Blue/red	£150-£200
	Blue/blue	£175-£225
	Black	£100-£150
	Pink	£125-£175
	Red	£400-£500
107	Sunbeam Alpine (CF)	£70-£80
108	MG Midget (CF)	£100-£130
109	Austin Healey Sprite (CF)	£70-£80
110	Aston Martin DB5	£70-£80
111	Triumph TR2 (CF) Pink	£80-£100
	Turquoise	£80-£100
112	Austin Healey Sprite	£70-£80
	South African Issues	£250-£300
113	MGB	£80-£90
	South African Issues	£250-£350
114	Triumph Spitfire	£70-£120
115	Plymouth Fury Sports	£70-£100
116	Volvo 1800s	
120	Jaguar 'E' Type	£60-£70
	(Red body not blue as shown)	
122	Volvo Estate	£10-£15
123	Austin Princess	£10-£15
124	RR Phantom	£15-£20
127	RR Silver Cloud	£60-£80
128	Mercedes Benz 600	£35-£45
128	Mercedes Benz 600	£20-£30
129	1300 V.W. Sedan	£40-£50
130	Ford Corsair	£50-£70
131	Cadillac Elderado	£70-£90
132	Jaguar 'E' Type	£70-£90
	Speedwheels Issue	£40-£50
132	Packard Convertible	£70-£90
132	Ford 40 RV	£40-50
133	Cunningham C5R	£70--£90
133	Ford Cortina	£30-£40
134	Triumph Vitesse	£45-£60
135	Triumph 2000	£50-£60
	Delete reference to Black body replace with metallic blue	£100-£120
136	Vauxhall Viva	
	metallic blue (shades)	£35-£50
	Off-white	£50-£70
137	Plymouth Fury Convertible	
	Pink and Metallic Green	£70-£80
138	Hillman Imp	£30-£40
139a	Ford Fordor	£50-£70
	add £20-£30 for box	
139b	Hudson	£50-£70
	add £20-£30 for box	
139	Ford Cortina	£50-£60
140	Morris 1100	£40-£50

Auction Price Result
140b Rover 75, 2 blue, 2 blue/cream, 2 cream
      in half dozen trade box (E-M)   *Phillips*   £280

141	Vauxhall Victor Estate Car	
	Yellow	£40-£50
	Pink	£250-£300
142	Jaguar MK10	£40-£50
143	Ford Capri	£40-£50
144	Volkswagon 1500	£40-£50
145	Singer Vogue	£50-£70
146	Daimler 2½ litre V8	£50-£70
147	Cadillac 62	£50-£70
148	Ford Fairlane	
	Green	£50-£70
	Metallic Green	£150-£200
	South African Issues	£250-£300
149	Citroen Dyane	£20-£25
150	RR Silver Wraith	£50-£60
151	(40b) Triumph 1800	£80-£100
151	Vauxhall Victor 101	£25-£35
152	RR Phantom	£25-£35
	Metallic Blue	£15-£25
152	(40d) Austin Devon	£80-£100
	Blue/Yellow or Grey/Pink	£150-£200
	Green/Cerise	£250-£300
153	Standard Vanguard	£80-£100
153	Aston Martin	£50-£60
154	Hillman Minx	
	Green Brown	£800-£100
	Green/Cream	£115-£135
	Pink/Blue	£150-£200
154	Ford Taunus	£30-£40
155	Ford Anglia	£50-£60
	South African Issues	£250-£300
156	Rover 75	
	Cream body	£80-£100
	Blue/Cream or TT Blue	£125-£150
156	Saab 96	£60-£80
157	Jaguar XK 120	
	Red or green	£95-£115
	White or yellow	£120-£140
	Red//Green	£140-£170
	Yellow/Grey	£160-£200
157	(BMW) 2000	£40-£50
158	Riley Saloon	£80-£100
158	Rolls Royce Silver Shadow	
	Red body	£30-£40
	Metallic blue	£15-£25
159	Morris Oxford	
	Fawn or green	£80-£100
	Green/cream	£120-£150
	Red/white	£150-£200
159	Ford Cortina	£50-£60
160	Mercedes Benz 250 SE	£40-£50
160	Austin A30	£70-£80
161	Austin Somerset	
	Red or light blue	£80-£100
	Black/cream	£150-£160
	Yellow/red	£180-£200
	Blue/cerise	£250-£300

161	Ford Mustang	£30-£40	179	Opel Commodore		£30-£40
162	Ford Zephyr		180	Packard Clipper		£70-£90
	Cream/green	£90-£110	180	Rover 3500		£15-£20
	Two tone blue	£90-£110	180	Volvo Estate		£10-£15
162	Triumph 1300	£40-£50	181	VW Saloon		
163	Bristol 450	£40-£50		Blue or Grey		£50-£60
163	VW 1600 TL	£40-£50		South African Issues		£200-£250
164	Vauxhall Cresta		182	Porsche 356A Coupe		
	Maroon/cream	£90-£110		Pale blue, cream or red		£80-£100
	Green/black	£60-£70		Dusty Pink		£250-£300
165	Ford Capri	£25-£35	183	Fiat 600		£60-£70
166	Sunbeam Rapier	£70-£80	183	Morris Mini		£40-£50

				South African		£200-£250
166	Renault R16	£25-£35	184	Volvo 122S		£50-£60
167	A.C. Aceca	£70-£90	185	Alfa Romeo 1900		£50-£60
168	Singer Gazelle		186	Mercedes 220 SE		£30-£40
	Cream/brown	£90-£120	187	VW Karmann Ghia Coupe		£60-£80
	Grey/green	£70-£90	188	Jensen FF		£30-£40
168	Ford Escort	£25-£40	189	Triumph Herald		£45-£60
169	Studebaker Golden Hawk	£60-£70	189	Lamborghini Marzal		£25-£30
169	Ford Corsair 2000E	£40-£50	190	Monteverdi 325 1		£25-£30
170	Ford Fordor		191	Dodge Royal Sedan		£80-£90
	Yellow or red	£80-£100	192	De Soto Fire Flite		£80-£90
	Red/cream or Pink/blue	£150-£200	192	Range Rover		£15-£20
170	Lincoln Continental	£40-£60	193	Nash Rambler		£40-£50
170	Granada never released			South African Issues		£200-£250
	Six models known to exist, red and blue examples in Chester Toy Museum		194	Bentley 'S' Coupe		
171	(1396) Hudson Commodore Sedan			Grey		£50-£60
	Cream or Dark Red	£80-£100		Gold		£70-£80
	Blue/grey, Cream/maroon	£115-£145		South African Issues		£100-£200
	Blue/fawn or Red/turquoise	£115-£145	195	Jaguar 3.4 MKII		£50-£70
171	Austin 1800	£40-£50	196	Holden Special Sedan		
172	Studebaker Land Cruiser			Bronze/white		£45-£65
	Green or Blue	£80-£100		Blue/white		£45-£65
	Beige/cream or White/pink	£120-£150		South African		£150-£200
172	Fiat 2300 Station Wagon	£40-£50	197	Morris Traveller		£40-£50
173	Nash Rambler	£60-£70	198	Rolls Royce Phantom V		
173	Pontiac Parisienne	£50-£60		Fluorescent colours		£80-£90
174	Hudson Hornet	£70-£90		Two tone grey		£60-£80
174	Ford Mercury Cougar	£35-£45		Green/cream		£50-£60
175	Hillman Minx		199	Mini Countryman		£40-£50
	Yellow/grey	£125-£150	200	Midget Racer		£30-£40
	Grey/blue or Blue/turquoise	£100-£125	200	Matra Le Mans		£15-£25
	Beige/cream	£80-£100	201	Plymouth Stock Car		£15-£25
175	Cadillac Eldorado	£50-£60	202	Fiat Abarth		£15-£25
176	Austin A105 Saloon		202	Land Rover		£15-£20
	Grey/Red or Cream/Blue	£80-£100	202	Land Rover		£15-£20
	Black/cream	£250-£300	203	Land Rover		£15-£20
176	N.S.U. R80	£40-£50	204	Ferrari 312P		£20-£25
177	Opel Kapitan	£30-£40	205	Talbot Lago		£60-£70
	South African Issues	£150-£200	205	Lotus Cortina Rally		£60-£70
178	Plymouth Plaza		206	Maserati		£60-£70
	Pale blue/white	£140-£180	206	Sting Ray		£20-£25
	Pink/green	£80-£100	207	Alfa Romeo		£60-£70
	Two tone blue	£70-£90	207	Triumph TR7 Rally		£20-£25
178	Mini Clubman	£15-£25	208	Cooper Bristol		£60-£70
179	Studebaker President	£80-£100	208	VW Porsche 914		£20-£25
			209	Ferrari		£60-£70
			210	Vanwall		£60-£70
			210	Alfa Romeo 35		£20-£25
			211	Triumph TR7		£20-£25

212	Ford Cortina Rally	£50-£60
213	Ford Capri Rally	£40-£50
214	Hillman Imp Rally	£40-£50
215	Ford GT Racer	£30-£40
216	Dino Ferrari	£20-£25
217	Alfa Scarabeo	£15-£25
218	Lotus Europa	£30-£40
219	Leyland Jaguar	NGPP
219	Jaguar XJ 5 Litre Big Cat	£10-£15
220	(23a) Racing Cars	£20-£30
220	Ferrari P5	£15-£20
221	(23c) Speed of wind	£30-£40
221	Corvette Sting Ray	£20-£25
222	(23s) Streamlined Racing Car	£30-£40
222	Hesketh 308E	£10-£15
223	Mclaren M8A Can-Am	£15-£20
224	Mercedes CH1	£15-£20
225	Lotus F1	£15-£20
226	Ferrari 312/B2	£10-£15
227	Beach Buggy	£15-£20
228	Super Sprinter	£15-£20
230	(23k) Talbot Lago	£50-£60
231	(23n) Maserati	£50-£60
232	(23p) Alfa Romeo	£50-£60

233	(23q) Cooper Bristol	£50-£60
234	(23h) Ferrari	£50-£60
	with yellow triangle on nose	£80-£90
235	(23j) H.W.M.	£50-£60
236	Connaught	£50-£60
237	Mercedes (yellow or blue driver)	£50-£60
238	'D' type Jaguar	£50-£60
239	Vanwall	£50-£60
240	Cooper Bristol	£30-£40
241	Lotus	£30-£40
242	Ferrari	£30-£40
243	B.R.M.	£30-£40
262	VW Swiss Post (Closed doors)	£150-£200
	Opening doors issue	£25-£35
342	Austin Mini Moke	£20-£25
344	Land Rover	£20-£25
405	Universal Jeep	£40-£50
518	Renault	£50-£60
5635	Citreon 2CV	£50-£60
550	Chrysler Saratoga	£80-£100
553	Peugeot 404	£50-£60
555	Ford Thunderbird	£70-£80

N.B. Enhance the prices of models not listed by 15%

Gift Sets

22 Series	£2000-£2500
23 Series	£400-£500
24 Series	£3500-£4000
30 Series	£2500-£3000
35 Series	£4000-£5000
36 Series	£3500-£4000
38 Series	£1500-£2000
39 Series	£2000-£3000

Previously unrecorded set:-
Dinky Set No. 2
 1946-48 Private Automobiles Set.
 Sold by Lacy Scott May 1989, set includes
 39a Packard (Green), 39b Oldsmobile (Grey),
 39c Lincoln Zephyr (Grey), 39d Buick
 (Maroon), 39e Chrysler Royal (Blue)
 See illustration   £1900

Dinky Set No. 3		£750-£850
N.B. Listing should read, 40e and not 40c		
Dinky Set No. 4 Racing Cars		£500-£700
118	Glider Set	£150-£180
121	Goodwood Set	£650-£750
N.B. Includes 9 figures plus driver in No. 113		
122	Touring Set	£650-£750
123	Mayfair Set	£650-£800
124	Holiday Set	£350-£400
125	Fun-A-Hoy Set	£180-£250
126	Motor Show Set	£450-£500
149	Sports Cars Set (add 109 to listing)	£650-£750
201	Racing Cars Set	£350-£450
245	Superfast Set	£100-£150
246	International Set	£100-£150
950	Car Transporter Set	
	(believed never released)	
990	Car Transporter Set	£750-£850

Collectors Notes

Original Dinky Toys Press Photo.
No. 176 N.S.U. RO 80 Battery powered models.

Dinky Commercial and Utility Vehicles

22 SERIES

22c	Motor Truck	£250-£350
22c	Motor Truck	£100-£150
22c	Motor Truck	£50-£70

25 SERIES

25b	'Meccano'	£200-£250
25d	All pre war Tankers	£100-£150

Pristine examples are priced 30% — 50% higher

Auction Price Results

25c	Covered wagon in half dozen trade box cream/red canopy and hubs 3rd type (G-E)	*Phillips*	£200
25d	Petrol Tank Wagon 1st type, 1 green, 1 red, 2nd type 4 green in half dozen trade box (E)	*Phillips*	£200
25a	Wagon 1st type (5) 2nd type (1) in half dozen trade box blue, light and dark green, light and dark grey (E)	*Phillips*	£170
25f	Market Gardeners Wagon various colours 1st type (3), 2nd type (1) in Trade Box (G-E)		£110
25l	Fire Engine six in half dozen trade box (E-M)	*Phillips*	£240

25x	Commer Breakdown Lorry		
	Light Brown/green Unboxed		£40-£50
	Grey/blue Unboxed		£60-£70
	Cream/blue Unboxed		£150-£170
	Red/grey Unboxed		£150-£170

30 SERIES

30j	(343) Austin Wagon (unboxed)		£30-£40
30e	Breakdown Lorry (unboxed)		£60-£80
30e	Breakdown Lorry (unboxed)		£35-£40
30m	Rear Tipper		£50-£60
30n	Farm Produce Wagon		£60-£70
30p	(440) (unboxed)	'MOBILGAS'	£40-£50
30pa	(441) (unboxed)	'CASTROL'	£40-£50
30pb	(442) (unboxed)	'ESSO'	£40-£50
30r	(422) (unboxed) Fordson Thames Truck		£30-£40
30s	(413) (unboxed) Austin Covered Wagon		£40-£50
60y	Thomson Aircraft Tender		£350-£450
107a	Sack Truck Delete-See Farm and Garden		
252	(25v) Refuse Truck		£70-£100
252	Refuse Truck		£90-£120
	With Green/black shutters		£300-£400
	With Orange/grey/green shutters		£250-£300
402	Bedford Lorry		£150-£175
408	(922) Big Bedford Lorry		
	— Maroon/fawn		£80-£100
	— Blue/yellow		£100-£125
409	(921) Bedford Articulated Vehicle		
	— Yellow/black		£90-£120
410	(25m) Bedford End Tipper		
	—Blue/yellow		£90-£110
	—Red/cream		£80/£100
	Delete Brown/yellow		
411	(25W) Bedford Truck		£80-£100

413	Austin Covered Wagon		
	Blue with pale blue canopy and hubs		£80-£90
	Maroon with tan canopy and red hubs		£80-£90
	Pale blue with cream canopy and hubs		£200-£250
501	Foden 8 Wheel Diesel Wagon		£250-£300
501	(901) Foden 8 Wheel Diesel Wagon		£250-£350
502	Foden Flat Truck		£250-£350
502	(902) Foden Flat Truck		£100-£200
503	(903) Foden with Tailboard		£250-£350
504	Foden Tanker (Grey/Red)		£200-£250
504	Foden Tanker (TT Blue)		£150-£200
504	(941) 'MOBILGAS'		£600-£700
505	(905) Foden Chain Lorry Cab		
	Maroon (1st)		£1500-£1700
	Green (1st)		£600-£800
	2nd cab with either colour		£200-£250
511	(911/431) Guy Lorry		£200-£250
512	(912/432) Guy Flat		£200-£250
513	(913/433) Guy with Tailboard		£200-£250
521	Bedford Articulated Vehicle		
	Yellow/black		£90-£120
	Maroon/fawn		£80-£100
	Dark red/black (new entry)		£180-£200
522	(922/408) Big Bedford		£100-£125
531	(931/417) Leyland Comet (Slatted sides)		£100-£125
532	(932/418) Leyland Comet (Tailboard) (New colour variation green/red with cream hubs)		£125-£150
571	(971) Coles Crane		£35-£45
579	Simca Glaziers Lorry	Grey/green	£80-£100
		Yellow/green	£70-£80
581	Berliot Flat Truck		£60-£70
581	Racehorse Transport		£70-£90
581	US Issue Racehorse Transport		£500-£600
582	(982) Pullmore Transporter		£60-£80
	All Dark Blue Issue		£150-£250
591	A.E.C. Tanker		£150-£170
908	Mighty Antar with Transporter		£350-£450
914	A.E.C. Articulated Vehicle		£100-£125
915	A.E.C. with Flat Trailer		£60-£70
934	Leyland Octopus Wagon		
	Yellow/green		£145-£175
	Blue/cream		£1000-£1500
935	Leyland Octopus with Chains		
	Green/cream		£800-£1000
	Blue/cream		£1000-£1500
936	Leyland 8 Wheel Chassis		£70-£90
942	Foden Tanker 'REGENT'		£350-£500
943	Leyland Octopus Tanker 'ESSO'		£300-£400
944	Leyland Octopus 4000 gal Tanker		£200-£250
945	A.E.C. Fuel Tanker 'ESSO'		
	1st issue with rear 'tiger' label		£70-£90
	2nd issue		£40-£50
945	A.E.C. Fuel Tanker 'LUCAS'		£60-£80
950	Foden Tanker 'BURMAH'		£40-£50
950	Foden Tanker 'SHELL'		£70-£80
958	Guy Warrior Snow Plough		£180-£200
967	BBC TV Control Room		£85-£100

968	BBC TV Roving Eye	£65-£85	
969	BBC TV Extending Mast	£85-£100	
970	Jones Cantilever Crane		
	Yellow body	£35-£50	
	Red (new entry)	£50-£60	
974	A.E.C. Hoyner Transporter	£70-£80	
977	Servicing Platform Vehicle	£200-£250	
978	Bedford Refuse Vehicle		
	1st issue Green/grey	£50-£60	
	2nd issue Metallic Green or Lime Green	£25-£40	
983	Car Carrier and Trailer	£150-£200	
986	Mighty Antar with Propellor	£175-£225	
987	TV Control Room 'ABC'	£125-£150	
988	TV Transmitter Van 'ABC'	£140-£170	
989	Car Transporter	£1500-£2000	

N.B. Enhance the prices of any models not included by 20%

Page 63 Amendment to information on castings D. The Heavy Commercial Types 1947-60. Due to a printing error the diagrams for the 1st type Guy 1947-54 and the Warrior type 1956-60 have been reversed, please amend your catalogue accordingly. N.B. Shown correctly in this Issue.

Auction Price Results

Phillips West Two London Auction
December 1988 and May 1989

502	Foden Flat Truck (Green) (M) boxed	£380
503	Foden with Tailboard (Orange/blue) (M) boxed	£300
504	Foden Tanker (Red/grey) (M) boxed	£420
504	Foden Tanker (TT Blue) (M) boxed	£300
505	Foden Flat 1st type cab (E) green	£700

505	Foden Flat with Chains (TT Green) (M) boxed	£320
505	Foden Flat with Chains (Red/grey) (M) boxed	£380
511	Guy 4 ton Lorry (TT Blue) (E) boxed	£120
511	Guy 4 ton Lorry (Grey/red) (E-M) boxed	£220
512	Guy Flat Truck (Red/blue) (E) boxed	£110
512	Guy Flat Truck (Brown/green((M) boxed	£500
513	Guy with Tailboard (TT Green) (M) boxed	£160
591	A.E.C. Tanker	£190
902	Foden Flat Truck (Orange/green)	£240
908	Mighty Antar with Transformer	£650
933	Leyland Cement Wagon	£140
934	Leyland Octopus Wagon (Yellow/green)	£420
935	Leyland Octopus Flat Truck with Chains Unboxed (G-E) Blue/green	£700
941	Foden 14 ton Tanker 'MOBILGAS'	£650
532	Leyland Comet Wagon with Hinged Tailboard	
	Green/red with cream hubs (M) boxed	£300
522	Big Bedford Lorry (Yellow/blue) (M) boxed	£220
581	Horse Box 'BR' (M) boxed	£120
942	Foden 14 ton Tanker 'REGENT' (M) boxed	£450
943	Leyland Octopus Tanker 'ESSO' (E-M) boxed	£380
944	Leyland Octopus 'BP' Tanker (E) boxed	£220
979	Racehorse Transporter (M) boxed	£300
983	Car Carrier and Trailer (M) boxed	£260
987	ABC Control Room (E-M) boxed	£200

Dinky Vans

28 SERIES
1st, 2nd and 3rd Issues
Increase listed prices by 20%

Auction Price Result

	New entry 280 series type 2 promotional model 'Maison de Bonneterie, Amsterdam Den Haag.	*(Phillips)*	
	Maroon with gold logo (G)		£750
31a	(450) Trojan Van 'Esso' half dozen in Trade Box	*(Phillips)*	£340
31	Holland Coachcraft Van		£250-£350
31a	Trojan Van 'ESSO'		£110-£125
31b	Trojan Van 'DUNLOP'		£115-£135
31c	Trojan Van 'CHIVERS'		£125-£150
31d	Trojan Van 'OXO' (unboxed)		£200-£250
34a	'ROYAL AIR MAIL SERVICE' Car		£250-£300
34b	'ROYAL MAIL'		£80-£90
34c	Loudspeaker Van — Colours Blue, Green, Grey or Brown (unboxed)		£25-£40
260	'ROYAL MAIL' Van		£80-£110
261	Post Office Van		£70-£90
273	R.A.C. Mini Minor	1st	£80-£100
		2nd	£60-£70
274	A.A. Mini Minor	1st	£80-£100
		2nd	£60-£70

274	Mini Minor Van 'MASONS PAINTS' promotional issue (with leaflet in red box)		£600-£700
275	Brinks Armoured Car	1st	£80-£100
		2nd	£35-£45
		Mexican	£1000-£1250
280	Mobile Midland Bank		£65-£85
407	Ford Transit 'KENWOOD'		£45-£60
407	Ford Transit 'HEINZ'		£45-£60
416	"1000,000 TRANSITS" rare issue		NGPP
450	Bedford 'Tk' Van 'CASTROL'		£150-£200
455	Trojan Van 'BROOKE BOND'		£150-£175
465	Morris 10 aut Van 'CAPSTAN'		£150-£200
470	Austin A40 Van 'SHELL'		£80-£100
471	Austin A40 Van 'NESTLES'		£90-£110
472	Austin A40 Van 'RALEIGH'		£90-£110
480	Bedford Van 'KODAK'		£80-£100
481	Bedford Van 'OVALTINE'		£80-£100
482	Bedford Van 'DINKY TOYS'		£100-£150
514	Guy Van 'SLUMBERLAND'		£300-£350
514	Guy Van 'LYONS SWISS ROLLS'		£800-£1000
514	Guy Van 'WEETABIX'		£1800-£2000
514	Guy Van 'SPRATTS'		£300-£450
918	Guy Van 'EVER READY'		£250-£300
919	Guy Van 'GOLDEN SHRED'		£600-£800
920	Guy Warrior 'HEINZ KETCHUP'		£1750-£2000

923	Big Bedford 'HEINZ BEANS'	£250-£300
923	Big Bedford 'HEINZ KETCHUP'	£800-£1000
930	Bedford Pallet Van	£250-£300

Gift Sets

28 SERIES 28/1		£5000-£6000
New Entry Postal Set No. 12		
Contains 34b, 12a, 12b, 12c, 12d, 12e		£600-£700

N.B. Enhance the prices of any models not included by 20%

Auction Price Results

Phillips West Two London December 1988

No. 12	Postal Set (E-M) slight fatigue	£650
450	Trojan Van 'ESSO' (M) boxed	£230
452	Trojan Van 'CHIVERS' (M) boxed	£240
455	Trojan Van 'BROOKE BOND' (M) boxed	£260
465	Morris 10 cwt Van 'CAPSTAN' (M) boxed	£130
490	Electric Dairy Van (Grey/blue) 'EXPRESS'	£55

490	Electric Dairy Van (Cream/red) 'EXPRESS' (M) boxed	£75
491	Electric Dairy Van 'JOB'S' (M) boxed	£80
491	Half dozen in Trade Box 'JOB'S' (individually boxed)	£420
492	Loudspeaker Van (M) boxed	£65
514	Guy Van 'SLUMBERLAND' (M) boxed	£420
514	Guy Van 'WEETABIX' (E-M) boxed	£1400
514	Guy Van 'LYONS SWISS ROLLS' (E-M) boxed	£1700
917	Guy Van 'SPRATTS' (M) boxed	£550
918	Guy Van 'EVER READY' (M) boxed	£380
919	Guy Van 'GOLDEN SHRED' (M) boxed	£1000
923	Big Bedford 'HEINZ KETCHUP' (E-M) boxed	£1400
923	Big Bedford 'HEINZ BEANS' (M) boxed	£200

Gift Set

523	Post Office Services Set	£600

Collectors Notes

Dinky Fire, Police and Ambulance Vehicles

Original Dinky Toys Press Photo
No. 285 Merryweather Marquis Fire Engine — finger on the pump button!

24a	1934-38 Ambulance	£125-£150
25k	1936-40 Streamlined Fire Engine	£100-£125
25k	1938-40 Streamlined Fire Engine	£150-£200
30f	1935-38 Ambulance (Red Crosses)	£125-£150
30f	1938-40 Ambulance (Red Crosses)	£100-£125
30f	1947-48 Ambulance (Red Crosses)	£90-£110
30f	1948-50 Ambulance (Red Crosses)	£70-£90
30l	Daimler Ambulance (unboxed)	£40-£50
250	(25h) Streamlined Fire Engine	£60-£80
251	U.S.A. Police Car	£25-£40
253	(30) Daimler Ambulance	£50-£70
	Available in cream and white (new entry)	£50-£70
255	Mersey Tunnel Police	£45-£65
255	Ford Zodiac Police Car	£45-£65
257	Nash Rambler Fire Chief	£45-£60

258	USA 'POLICE' De Soto Fireflite	£65-£75
258	USA 'POLICE' Dodge Royal Sedan	£65-£75
258	USA 'POLICE' Ford Fairlane	£65-£75
259	1962-68 Bedford Miles Fire Engine (New Entry) Red body, ladder, bell 'Fire Brigade'	£60-£80
264	R.C.M.P. Ford Fairlane (New Entry)	£65-£75
265	R.C.M.P. Cadillac Version (New Ref. No.)	£50-£60
269	Jaguar Motorway Police Car	£70-£80
271	Ford Transit 'Fire'	£40-£50
276	Bedford Miles Airport Tender (Improved description)	
	with cab crest	£55-£65
	without crest	£45-£55

277	Superior Criterion Ambulance	£45-£50
278	Vauxhall Victor Ambulance	£45-£60
286	Ford Transit Fire Engine	£40-£50
555	Commer Fire Engine (Improved details)	
	Silver Ladder	£60-£70
	Brown Ladder	£80-£90

Auction Price Results

Phillips West Two London December 1988

253	Daimler Ambulance Cream and White (M) boxed (2)	£90
258	U.S.A. Police De Soto Fireflite (M) boxed	£65
264	R.C.M.P. Patrol Car (M) boxed	£75
265	R.C.M.P. Patrol Car (M) boxed	£55
276	Airport Fire Tender (M) boxed	£50
277	Superior Criterion Ambulance (M) boxed	£60

955	Renumbered from 555	
	with or without windows	£60-£80
956	Bedford 'S' type Turntable Fire Escape	
	Small Cab	£75-£90
	Large Cab	£125-£150
2253	Ford Capri Police Car	£35-£45

Gift Sets

294	Police Vehicles Set (250,254, 272)	£60-£80
297	Police Vehicles Set (200, 254, 287)	£100-£125
298	Emergency Services Set	£250-£350
299	Motorway Services Set	£250-£350
299	Crash Squad Set	£20-£30
302	Emergency Squad Set	£40-£50
304	Fire Rescue Set	£35-£50
957	Fire Services Set	£250-£350

N.B. Enhance prices of models not listed by 10%

Dinky Novelty, Space and Film/TV Link Up Models

100	Lady Penelope Fab 1	£125-£150
101	Thunderbird 2 and 4	£100-£125
102	Joes Car	£50-£70
103	Spectrum Patrol Car,	
	Red, yellow base	£80-£100
	Metallic Red, White base	£60-£80
	Gold body, blue tinted windows	£60-£70
104	Spectrum Pursuit Car	£70-£80
05	Maximum Security	£80-£100
106	Prisoner Mini Moke	£150-£200
106	Thunderbird 2 and 4	
	Blue all metal body	£40-£50
	Black plastic base	£35-£45
	White plastic base	£30-£40
107	Stripey the Magic Mini	£150-£200
108	Sams Car	
	Silver body	£40-£50
	Gold body	£80-£100
	Metallic Red	£30-£40
	Pale Blue	£50-£60
109	Gabriel Model 'T' Ford	£30-£40
111	Cinderella Coach	£10-£15
112	Purdey's TR7	£20-£30
115	United Biscuits 'TAXI'	£15-£20
120	Happy Cab	£15-£20
267	Paramount Truck	£25-£30
281	'PATHE NEWS' Car	£80-£100
350	Tiny's Mini Moke	£40-£50
351	U.F.O. Interceptor	£25-£40
352	Ed Strakers Car	
	Gold	£40-£50
	Red	£30-£50
	Yellow	£20-£30

353	Shado 2 Mobile	
	Delete Metallic Green	
	Listing should read Dark Green	£25-£40
	with metallic Dark Blue body	£40-£50
354	Pink Panther — with motor	£25-£30
	— without motor	£15-£20
355	Lunar Roving Vehicle	£25-£30
357	Klingon Battle Cruiser	£15-£20
358	USS Enterprise	£25-£35
359	Eagle Transporter	£25-£35
360	Eagle Freighter	
	White body, metallic blue pads and nose	£30-£35
	Metallic green pods and nose	£40-£50

N.B. Freight module in white or red can be inter-changed

361	Galactic War Chariot	£15-£20
362	Trident Star Fighter	£15-£20
363	Zygon Patroller	£20-£30
364	Space Shuttle	£40-£50
367	Space Battle Cruiser	£25-£35
368	Zygon Marander	£15-£25
368	Cosmic Cruiser	£60-£70
370	Dragster — white blue or red launcher	£20-£30
371	USS Enterprise	£40-£50
372	Klingon Cruiser	£40-£50
475	Model 'T' Ford	£40-£50
476	Morris Oxford 'BULLNOSE'	£60-£70
477	Parsley's Car	£80-£100
485	Santa Special Model 'T' Ford	£70-£80
486	Dinky Beats Morris Bullnose	£70-£80
602	Armoured Command Car	£25-£35
803	USS Enterprise	£40-£50
804	Klingon	£40-£50

Gift Set

309		£40-£50

Dinky Farm and Garden Models

22c	New Colour variant - Dark blue and yellow body with red wheels	£125-£195
27a	(300) Massey Harris Tractor (unboxed)	£30-£40
27h	Disc Harrow Red/yellow (unboxed)	£5-£10
27m	(301) Field Marshall Tractor (unboxed)	£45-£55
30m	Farm Produce Wagon (unboxed)	£35-£50
107a	(385) Sack Truck	£5-£10
300	Massey Harris Tractor (Both issues)	£50-£60
308	Leyland '384' Tractor Metallic Red	£40-£50
	Blue version	£25-£35
325	David Brown Tractor	£30-£40
342	Moto Cart	£50-£60
343	(30) Farm Produce Wagon	
	Red/blue	£50-£60
	Green/yellow	£50-£60

564	Elevator Loader	£25-£40

Auction Price Results

Phillips West Two London December 1988

381	Garden Roller Six in Trade Box (M)	£45
383	Hand Truck Six in Trade Box (M)	£40
385	Sack Truck Six in Trade Box	£80

N.B. Enhance prices for models not listed by 10%

New Entry

423	Large Trailer, Four in Trade Box	£100-£125

Gift Sets

Increase Listed Prices by 33%

Dinky Military Models

22f	Army Truck	£150-£175
225	Searchlight Lorry	£175-£225
25wm	Bedford Military Truck	£150-£250
30lm	Daimler Ambulance	£150-£250
30sm	Austin Covered Lorry	£150-£250
37c	Signals Despatch Rider	£40-£50
139am	US Army Staff Car	£150-£250
151a	Medium Tank	£80-£100
152a	1937-40 Light Tank	£60-£80
	46-48 Light Tank	£50-£60
152b	Reconnaissance Car	
	Gloss green (pre-war)	£60-£80
	Matt green or olive brown	£40-£50
152c	Austin Seven	£70-£80
161a	Searchlight on Lorry	£150-£200
162a	Light Dragon Tractor	£60-£70
162a	Light Dragon Tractor	£40-£50
170	Ford Fordor	£150-£200
616	A.E.C. with Chieftain Tank	£50-£60
618	A.E.C. with Helicopter	£40-£60
620	Berliet Missile Launcher	£70-£80
622	10 Ton Army Truck	£40-£50
623	Army Covered Wagon	£40-£50
624	Daimler Ambulance (US)	£200-£250
625	Austin Covered Lorry (US)	£200-£250
626	Military Ambulance	£40-£50
640	Bedford Truck (US)	£200-£250
642	RAF Pressure Refuller	£60-£80
650	Light Tank	£50-£60
660	Tank Transporter	£60-£70
661	Recovery Tractor	£60-£70
665	Honest John Missile Launcher	£45-£60

666	Missile Erector Vehicle	£125-£150
667	Missile Servicing Platform Vehicle	£100-£125
669	U.S.A. Universal Jeep (US)	£200-£250
689	Medium Artillery Tractor	£60-£70
690	Mobile A.A. Gun (US Issue)	£60-£70
691	Field Gun Unit (US Issue)	£100-£150
*815	Packard Armoured Tank	£45-£60
*817	AMX 13 ton Tank	£45-£60
*822	Half Track M3	£50-£70
*884	Brockway Bridge Truck	£180-£200
	*French issues released in the UK	

Gift Sets

150	Series	£70-£90
151	Series	£300-£400
152	Series amend to read:-	
	152 a,b,c plus 150d	
156	Series	£250-£1200
160	Series	£65-£75
161	Series	£350-£450
162	Series	£125-£150
303	Commando Set	£70-£80
606	Royal Artillery Personnel	£60-£70
677	Task Force Set	£25-£35
695	Howitzer/Trooper Set	£60-£80
697	25 pdr Field Gun Set	£50-£70
698	Tank Transporter Set	£70-£90
699	Military Vehicles Set	£175-£200

Auction Price Result

Phillips December 1988

665	Honest John ML (M) boxed	£65
675	Ford Fordor (US Issue) (M) boxed	£225
698	Tank Transporter Set (E) boxed	£110

Original Dinky Toys Press Photo
No. 731 S.E.P.E.C.A.T. Jaguar

60a	Imperial Airways Liner	£200-£250	
60a	Imperial Airways Liner	£200-£250	
60k	1936 Percival Gull (Amy Mollinson's)	£200-£300	
60e	1934-1940 General Monospar Plane	£100-£150	
60f	1934-40 Cierva Autogiro	£150-£200	
60g	1935-40 D.H. Comet	£65-£85	
60h	Singapore Flying Boat	£150-£200	
60m	Four Engined Flying Boat	£150-£200	
60p	Gloucester Gladiator	£130-£170	
60r	1937-40 Empire Flying Boat	£125-£150	
60v	Armstrong Whitworth Bomber	£150-£200	
60w	1938-40 Flying Boat Clipper	£120-£150	
60w	46-48 Flying Boat	£70-£90	
60x	Atlantic Flying Boat	£200-£250	
62g	Flying Fortress	£100-£150	
629	Long Range Bomber	£60-£80	
62l	Hawker Hurricane	£70-£90	
62k	Kings Aeroplane	£175-£200	
62m	Airspeed Envoy	£75-£95	
62m	Light Transport	£40-£60	
62n	Junkers JU90 Airliner	£175-£225	
	(Add to listing Black Body, White Crosses)		

62p	Armstrong Whitworth Airliner	£100-£150	708	B.E.A. Viscount	£75-£90
62r	Albatross Airliner	£150-£200	710	Beechcraft Bonanza	£20-£30
62r	Four Engine Liner	£60-£80	727	German Phantom II	£35-£50
62t	Armstrong Whitworth Bomber	£150-£200	727	F-4K Phantom	£60-£70
63	Mayo Composite Airliner	£250-£300	729	Multi Role Aircraft	£35-£45
66a	Heavy Bomber	£350-£450	730	US Navy Phantom	£40-£50
66b	Dive Bomber	£250-£350	734	Supermarine Swift (not Spitfire)	£50-£60
67a	Junkers Heavy Bomber	£250-£350	734	P47 Thunderbolt	£60-£80
70e	(705) Viking Air Liner	£50-£80	74	Spitfire MK II	£40-£50
700	Spitfire Mark II	£60-£80	749	(992) Avro Vulcan Bomber	£1000-£1500
701	Shetland Flying Boat	£250-£350	997	Caravelle SE 210	£125-£150
702	(999) Comet Airliner	£75-£100	998	Bristol Britannia	£180-£250
706	'Air France' Viscount	£75-£100			

Gift Sets

60	1st type No registration letters	£1500-£2000	65	Passenger Set	£1500-£2250
	2nd type with registration letters	£1000-£1500	66	Wartime Camouflage Set	£3000-£5000
61	R.A.F. Set	£450-£650	68	Wartime Set	£2000-£3000
64	Wartime Set	£900-£1200			

Auction Price Results

Phillips West Two London December 1988

N.B. All models boxed, at time of sale

			62k	Kings Aeroplane (M)	£175
			62n	Junkers JU90 Air Liner	
60b	Leopard Moth G-ACPPT (Green) (E)	£80		Silver Finish 'D-Avre' (E)	£250
60l	Singapore Flying Boat (Slight fatigue)	£175		Black Body version (E)	£200
60r	Empire Flying Boat (Cheviot) (G)	£175	62p	Armstrong Whitworth Air Liner	£150
60s	Pair of camouflaged Spitfires (M)	£125	62r	Armstrong Whitworth Bomber	£175
60d	Half dozen Low Wing Monoplane in		62x	40 seat Airliner (E)	£125
	Trade Box (G-E)	£340	63	Mayo Composite (E-M)	£250
60v	Armstrong Whitworth Bomber (M)	£185	70c	Viking Airliner (E)	£70
60w	Clipper 3 Flying Boat (E-M)	£175	702	Comet Airliner (M)	£100

Gift Sets

Set No 41	RAF Aeroplanes	£700	Set No 68	Wartime Aircraft	**£6000**

Collectors Notes

Original Dinky Toys Press Photo
No. 283 'RED ARROW' Coach

27	'OVALTINE' Tram	£200-£250
27	'LIPTONS TEA' Tram	£200-£250
29	'MARMITE' Double Deck Bus	£175-£225
29b	1935-40 Streamline Bus	£60-£80
29b	48-50 Streamline Bus	£40-£80
29c	1938-40 'DUNLOP TYRES' Double Deck Bus	£175-£225
29c	1947-48 Double Decker No Adverts	£85-£95
29c	(290) 1948-54 Double Deck 'DUNLOP TYRES' (Unboxed)	£30-£40
29c	Single Deck Bus (Unboxed)	£30-£40
29f	Observation Coach (Unboxed)	£50-£60
29g	Luxury Coach	
	Blue with cream flash (Unboxed)	£60-£80
	Cream with blue flash (Unboxed)	£30-£40
	Cream with red flash (Unboxed)	£40-£50
	Maroon with cream flash (Unboxed)	£30-£40
	Brown with orange flash (Unboxed)	£60-£80
291	Duple Roadmaster Coach (Unboxed)	£30-£40
369	1938-41 Taxi	£70-£100
	46-49 Taxi	£40-£70
40h	(254) Taxi Blue or yellow	£60-£90
	Green/yellow	£50-£60
	Black (spun hubs)	£95-£120
265	Plymouth Taxi	£50-£60
266	Canadian Plymouth Taxi	£50-£60
268	Renault Dauphine Mini Cab	£60-£70
282	Duple Roadmaster Coach (Boxed)	
	Blue with silver flash	£50-£60
	Red with silver flash	£60-£80
	Yellow with red flash	£125-£150
	Light blue with green/cream	£125-£150
282	Austin 1800 Taxi	£75-£90
283	B.O.A.C. Coach	£60-£70
283	'RED ARROW' Single Deck Coach	
	Non Metallic Red body	£25-£30
	Metallic Red body	£35-£40

London Routemaster Bus Issues

289	London Routemaster Bus Issues	
i)	'TERN SHIRTS'	£75-£85
ii)	'SSSCHEPPES'	£65-£75
iii)	'FESTIVAL OF LONDON STORES'	£175-£200
iv)	'ESSO'	£20-£25
v)	'WOOLWORTHS'	£20-£25
vi)	'THOLLENBECKS'	£80-£100
vi)	'MADAME TUSSAUDS'	£75-£95
	with blue labels	£65-£75
290	(29c) Double Decker 'DUNLOP'	£80-£100
	with 3rd type radiator	£65-£75
291	Double Decker 'EXIDE'	£75-£90

Atlantean Bus Issues

291	'KENNING' all issues	£25-£40
292	'REGENT'	£70-£80
	'RIBBLE'	£90-£100
293	'BP'	£60-£70
	with ribbed roof	£90-£100
295	'YELLOW PAGES'	£40-£45
	Pale yellow type	£30-£35

297	Silver Jubilee	£20-£25
	Woolworth Silver Jubilee	£20-£25
949	Wayne School Bus	£150-£175
952	Vega Mayor Luxury Coach	
	Light grey	£80-£100
	White	£70-£80
953	Continental Touring Coach	£250-£300
961	Vega Mayor Coach PTT	£200-£250

Gift Set

300	London Scene	£40-£50

Auction Price Results

Phillips West Two London December 1988

29a	'Q' type Motor Bus 'Marmite' (G) half dozen in Trade Box (Yellow, silver roof)	£850
29c	(No adverts) half dozen in Trade Box (E)	£250
36g	Half dozen in Trade Box — Grey, Blue, Green, Maroon, yellow and red (E-M)	£1200

N.B. Increase prices of any models not listed by 15%

Dinky Trains and Trams

16	Silver Jubilee Silver/grey	£140-£170
	New Entry Blue/Dark blue	£175-£225
16	L.N.E.R.	£80-£120
16	British Rail 'BR'	£75-£90
17	Passenger Train	£200-£250
18	Goods Train	£200-£250
19	Mixed Goods	£200-£250
20	Passenger Train	£200-£250
21	Modelled Miniatures	
	Hornby Train Set	£200-£300
26	G.W.R. Rail Car	£80-£100

262	Diesel Rail Car	£80-£100
784	Goods Train	£35-£50
798	Express Passenger	£70-£90

Auction Price Result

*16	Silver Jubilee Silver Grey with fatigue (E)	£100
*16	Silver Jubilee Blue/Dark blue (E-M)	£240
*20	Passenger Train Set some fatigue (G-E)	£100
*21	Hornby Train Set (E-M)	£340
*	all boxed	

Dinky Ships

50a	Battle Cruiser 'HORD'	£40-£50
50b	Battle Cruiser 'NELSON'	£40-£50
50c	Cruiser 'EFFINGHAM'	£30-£40
50d	Cruiser York	£30-£40
50e	Cruiser 'DELHI'	£30-£40
50f	Destroyer 'BROKE' class	£20-£30
50j	Submarine 'K' class	£20-£30
50h	Destroyer 'X' class	£20-£30
51a	'UNITED STATES OF AMERICA' (boxed)	£50-£60
51b	'EUROPA'	£40-£50
51c	'REX'	£50-£70
51d	'EMPRESS OF BRITAIN'	£40-£50
51e	'STRATHAIRD'	£40-£50
51f	'QUEEN OF BERMUDA'	£70-£80
51g	BRITANNIA	£60-£70

52	'QUEEN MARY' (543) (boxed)	£60-£70
52a/b	'QUEEN MARY' (boxed)	£45-£55
52m	QUEEN MARY (boxed)	£40-£50
52a	QUEEN MARY (boxed)	£30-£40
52c	NORMANDIE (boxed)	£30-£50
53a	Battleship 'DUNKERQUE' (boxed)	£25-£35
796	Healey Sports Boat on Trailer	
	White body with either red, green or yellow deck	£25-£35
797	Healey Sports Boat without orange trailer	£15-£20

Gift Sets

50	Warship Set	£150-£200
51	Great Liners Set	£100-£200

Dinky Road Making Equipment

25p	(251) Aveling Barford (unboxed)	£15-£25	961	(561) Blaw Knox Bulldozer	
251	as above boxed	£30-£40		Red body	£40-£50
437	Muir Hill 2WL Loader (see 963 below)			Yellow/grey	£70-£80
	Red body	£25-£35		Rare issue with green/orange blade	NGPP
	Yellow	£15-£25		(Details of this model required please)	
563	(963) Blaw Knox Heavy Tractor		963	(563) Blaw Knox Heavy Tractor	
	Red or orange body	£40-£50		Red	£40-£50
959	Foden Dump Truck with Bulldozer			Orange	£50-£60
	Blade			Yellow	£80-£100
	Red body silver blade	£80-£100	965	Rear Dump Truck 'Terex'	£80-£100
	Red body with silver tipper	£100-£150	966	Marrel Multi Bucket Unit	£50-£70
960	Albion Concrete Mixer Lorry		975	Ruston Bucyrus Excavator	£150-£250
	with yellow/blue barrel	£50-£60			
	with grey/blue barrel	£60-£80	400	Building Site Set **Gift Set**	£400-£500

Increase prices of unlisted models by 10%

Dinky Miscellaneous
Dinky Dublo

061	Ford Prefect	£30-£40	069	Massey Harris Tractor	£30-£40
062	Singer Roadster	£40-£50	070	A.E.C. Tanker	£70-£80
063	Commer Van	£30-£40	071	VW Delivery Van	£60-£70
064	Austin Lorry	£25-£35	072	Bedford Truck	£40-£50
065	Morris Pick-up	£30-£40	073	Landrover/Horse	£50-£60
066	Bedford Flat Truck	£25-£30	076	L.B. Tractor/Trailer	£40-£50
067	Austin Taxi	£50-£60	078	L.B. Trailer	£15-£25
068	Royal Mail Van	£50-£70			

Motor Cycles

37a	Civilian	£50-£60	43b	R.A.C. Patrol	£25-£35
37a	Civilian	£25-£35	44b	A.A. Patrol	£50-£60
37b	Police	£50-£60	44b	A.A. Patrol	£25-£35
37b	Police	£25-£35	270	(44b) Rubber or plastic wheels £25-£35	
37c	Signals	£50-£60	271	TS Patrol	£70-£80
42b	Police Patrol	£50-£60			
42b	Police Patrol	£25-£35		**Gift Set**	
43b	R.A.C. Patrol	£50-£60		Dinky Way Set	£25-£35

Caravans

30g	Caravan	£50-£65	188	4 Berth	£25-£35
30g	Caravan	£40-£55	190	Caravan	£25-£35
117	4 Berth	£25-£35			

Large Scale Models

2162	Capri (Blue)	£35-£45	2253 Capri Police	£35-£45
2214	Capri Rally	£35-£45		

Convoy Series All prices to read £10-£15 Except 399 £20-£25 (Gift Set)

Action Kits Add £5 to List Price

Mini Dinky

10	Ford Corsair	£25-£30	22	Oldsmobile		£15-£20
11	Jaguar 'E' Type	£35-£50	23	Rover 2000		£25-£30
12	Corvette	£15-£20	24	Ferrari		£15-£20
13	Ferrari 250	£15-£20	25	Ford Zephyr 6		£25-£30
14	Chevy	£15-£20	26	Mercedes 250		£15-£20
15	RR Silver Shadow	£25-£30	27	Buick Riviera		£15-£20
16	Ford Mustang	£15-£20	28	Ferrari F.I.		£15-£20
17	Aston Martin	£25-£30	29	Ford F.I.		£15-£20
18	Mercedes 230	£15-£20	30	Volvo P1800		£30-£35
19	MGB	£35-£50	31	V.W. 1600		£25-£30
20	Cadillac	£15-£20	32	Vauxhall Cresta		£35-£40
21	Fiat 2300	£15-£20	33	Jaguar MKX		£35-£40

Dinky Cars — Hong Kong

001	Buick Riviera	£60-£70	005	Ford Thunderbird Coupe	£80-£100
002	Chevrolet Corvair Monza	£80-£100	006	Rambler Classic	£80-£100
003	Chevrolet Impala	£60-£70	008	Rover 3500 Saloon	£15-£20
004	Dodge Polara Cabriolet	£80-£100			

Airfix Dinky Models

Models 500 - 508 add £5 to list prices   Models 101 - 130 reduce prices to £3-5

Dinky Accessories — Pre-War

1	Station Staff	£100-£125	44a	A.A. Box	£70-£80
2	Farmyard Animals	£50-£70	45	Tinplate Garage	£150-£200
3	Passengers Set	£80-£100	46	Pavement Set (Printed grey cardboard)	£20-£30
4	Engineering Staff Set	£70-£80	47	12 Road Signs Set	£125-£150
5	Train and Hotel Staff	£70-£90	47a,b,c	Traffic Lights	£5 each
6	Shepherd Set	£80-£100	48	Filling Station/Garage	£180-£220
12a	GPO Pillar Box	£20-£30	49a	Bowser Petrol Pump	£20-£30
12b	Air Mail Pillar Box	£20-£30			
13	'Halls Distemper'	£70-£90			
13a	'Cooks' Man	£15-£20			
15	Railway Signals Set				
	Contains 15a,b,c signals £5-£10 each				
42a	Police Box	£20-£25			
42c	Policeman	£15-£20			
43a	R.A.C. Box	£70-£90			
40a	R.A.C. Guide Saluting	£15-£20			

Gift Sets

12 Series	£200-£250
42 Series	£80-£100
43 Series	£200-£250
44 Series	£200-£250
49 Series	£80-£100

Auction Price Result

13	Halls Distemper	*Phillips* £75

Post War Accessories

001	Station Staff	£50-£60	053	Passengers	£25-£30
002	Farmyard Animals	£40-£50	502	Garage	£75-£100
003	Passengers Set	£60-£80	752	Goods Yard Crane	£25-£40
004	Engineering Staff	£50-£60	753	Police Crossing	£75-£100
005	Train and Hotel Staff	£50-£60	766-	769 British Road Signs	£25-£30
006	Shepherd Set	£70-£80	772	British Road Signs (24)	£100--£125
007	Petrol Pump Attendants	£15-£20	780	Petrol Pump Set renumbered from 49 in	
008	Fire Station Personnel			1954	£50-£60
	(Packed in Printed Plastic Bag)	£25-£40	781	'ESSO', 782 'SHELL', 783 'BP'.	
009	Service Station Personnel	£25-£40		Petrol Pump Models	£35-£40
010	Road Maintenance Personnel	£40-£50	785	'Service Station' (337x185mm)	
013	Cook's Man Set of Six	£40-£50		Fawn/red plastic with windows and	
051	Station Staff	£25-£30		sliding doors	£80-£100

Dinky Toys — The Collection — New Issues

Manufactured by Matchbox International Ltd in Macau

DY1	1988	1967 Series 1½	"E' TYPE JAGUAR 4.2'	British Racing Green. RGN 'J916'
DY2	1989	1957 'Chevrolet'		Red body, white roof, silver side flash, RGN 'ASA174'
DY3	1989	1965 'MGB GT'		Teal blue body, black roof, RGN 'PBY 323C'
DY4	1989	1950 Ford E83W	10 cwt Van	Yellow body, black roof, 'HEINZ', RGN '618 APH'
DY5	1989	'1949 Ford 'V8 Pilot'		Black body, silver trim, RGN 'H0Y 712'
DY6	1989	1951 Volkswagon	Deluxe Saloon	Light blue body, grey roof, RGN '111A-46003'
DY8	1989	1948 Commer 8 cwt Van	'SHARPS' Toffees	Red body, gold/blue design, silver trim

Models planned for release late in 1989

DY7	1989	1959 Cadillac	Maroon/white body
DY9	1989	1949 Land Rover	Green body, cream canopy RGN 'EOP 999!
DY10	1989	Mercedes Konferenze Coach	Cream/black body

Collectors Notes

Original 'Lesney' Press Photo
Model 21 Foden Concrete Truck.

Abbreviations
GPW — Grey plastic wheels. SPW — Silver plastic wheels
BPW — Black plastic wheels.

3a	Cement Mixer GPW	£30-£40
4a	Massey Harris Tractor	£30-£35
4b	Massey Harris Tractor	£25-£30
7a	Horse Drawn Milk Float Metal wheels	£35-£45
8b	Caterpillar Tractor	£30-£40
8c	Ford Mustang (Orange)	£75-£100
9c	Fire Engine Tan Ladder	£15-£20
10d	Pipe Truck white base	£10-£15
11a	Tanker (Yellow)	£45-£55
13b	Wreck Truck GPW	£40-£50
16b	Atlantic Trailer (Tan)	£30-£40

17a	Bedford Removals Van	
	Blue	£55-£65
	Maroon	£55-£65
	Green	£30-£40
17c	Austin Taxi GPW	£20-£25
19b	MGA Sports SPW	£50-£60
19c	Aston Martin '52' decals	£30-£40
21c	Commer Milk Float	
	Bottle decals	£20-£25
	Cow decals	£15-£20
23b	Caravan (Pale Blue)	£20-£25
25cc	Bedford 'ARAL' Tanker	£55-£75
25d	Ford Cortina	
	Brown or Metallic Blue	£10-£15

30a	Ford Prefect (Blue) GPW	£100-£125
32a	Jaguar XK 140 (Red)	£100-£150
32c	Leyland 'ARAL' Tanker	£35-£45
35a	Horse Box SPW	£35-£45
36a	Austin A50 GPW	£20-£25
39a	Ford Zodiac Turquoise interior	£20-£25
39c	Ford Tractor (Orange)	£25-£35
43a	Hillman Minx (Green)	£100-£150
466	'PICKFORDS' Truck (Blue) 3 lines SPW	£50-£75
466	'BEALES-BEALSON' Truck	£150-£175
47c	'DAF' Container Truck (Yellow/turquoise)	£30-£40
51a	Commer Pickup (Red/grey) BPW	£35-£45
53a	Aston Martin (Red) BPW	£60-£70
56a	Trolley Bus BPW	£25-£30
59a	'SINGER' Van (Dark Green) SPW or GPW	£75-£100
60a	Morris J2 Pick Up	
	Red/Black logo	£25-£35
	Red/White logo	£15-£25
63a	Service Ambulance	£15-£20
66a	Citroen SPW	£40-£50
70b	Water Truck — Knobby or Fine Wheels	£30-£40

Add 15%—20% to all models not listed including the Gift Sets

Auction Price Results

Prices realised at Auction held by Phillips, 11 Salem Road, London W2 in March 1989. The figures in brackets indicates the number of models in the lot.

5a	London Bus 'BUY MATCHBOX' (2)	£75
5b	London Bus 'VISCOSTATIC' (2)	£80
7b	Ford Anglia grey plastic wheels	£75

9a	Dennis Fire Engine (2)	£75
10c	'TATE & LYLE' Truck (2)	£75
14b	Daimler Ambulance	£40
17a	Bedford Removal Van (Blue and a Green)	£100
17a	Bedford Removal Van (Maroon with gold radiator)	£80
17c	Austin Taxi (2)	£60
22a	Vauxhall Cresta colours as follows:-	
	Pale Pink	£70
	Bronze	£75
	Copper/Turquoise	£80
27c	Cadillac Sixty Special Purple Pink (2)	£80
29b	Austin Cambridge (2)	£75
30a	Ford Prefect (2)	£60
35a	Horse Box (3)	£75
38b	Vauxhall Victor	£35
39a	Ford Convertible(2)	£45
41a	Jaguar 'D' Type (2)	£75
43a	Hillman Minx (2) Turquoise/white and Blue/grey	£60
46a	Morris Minor Dark Green (2)	£75
53a	Aston Martin (2)	£40
56a	London Trolley Bus with silver headlights	£150
57a	Wolseley 1500 with black bumper	£60
58a	B.E.A. Coach — plain white lettering (3)	£75
58a	B.E.A. Coach — with red B.E.A. logo (3)	£120
66a	Citroen DS-19 yellow (3)	£75
74a	Mobile Refreshment Silver-Grey (2)	£110
G4	Farm Gift Set	£130

Major Series Models

M1a	Caterpillar Excavator	£20-£25	M5	'MASSEY FERGUSON' Combine	£20-£25
b	'BP' Petrol Tanker	£15-£20	M6a	'PICKFORDS' Transporter	£35-£40
M2a	Bedford 'WALLS ICE CREAM'	£30-£35	b	'BP' RACING TRANSPORTER'	£20-£25
b	York Trailer 'DAVIES'		M7	Jennings Cattle Truck	£20-£25
	Tyres	£15-£20	M8a	'MOBILGAS' Tanker	£35-£40
c	'LEP' Transport	£30-£35	b	'FARNBOROUGH MEASHAM'	£25-£30
M3	Centurion Transporter	£25-£30	M9	'COOPER JARRETT' Freighter	£40-£45
M4a	'RUSTON BUCYRUS'	£20-£25	M10	Dinkum Rear Dumper	£15-£20
b	'FREUHOF' Hopper Train	£30-£35			

Early Accessory Packs

1a	'ESSO' Petrol Pumps	£15-£20	3	Garage	£15-£20
1b	'BP' Petrol Pumps	£15-£20	4	Road Signs Set	£10-£15
2	'MATCHBOX CAR TRANSPORTER'	£30-£40	5	'HOME STORES'	£20-£25

Two Pack Models

This is a relatively small sector of the market place and the prices listed are unchanged

Matchbox 'King Size' Models

Main Price Changes

K1a Hydraulic Shovel	£20-£25	
K2a Dumper Truck	£20-£25	
K2b Dumper Truck	£20-£25	
K4b G.M.C. Tractor & Hoppers	£30-£35	
K7a Rear Dumper	£30-£35	
K8a Prime Mover/Crawler Tractor	£75-£100	

K9a Diesel Road Roller	£20-£25
K15a Merryweather Fire Engine	£25-£30
K20 Tractor Transporter	
Blue Tractor	£25-£30
Orange Tractors	£60-£75

Gift Sets

1963 King Size Set	£60-£70	1966 King Size Set	£40-£50
1965 Construction Set	£75-£85		

Early Lesney Toys

Please delete the following models which were incorrectly attributed to Lesney in the 3rd edition

vii)	Excavator	iv)	Caterpillar Tractor	£150-£175
viii)	Builders Crane	v)	Prime Mover	£500-£600
ix)	Small farm cart	vi)	Massey Harris Tractor	£300-£400
x)	Hayrake	vii)	Covered wagon with barrels	£300-£400
xvii)	Scooter and rider	viii)	Covered wagon without barrels	£300-£400
Peregrine Puppet and Red Drummer Boy		ix)	Merchants Cart	£1200-£1500
		x)	Soap Box Racer	£2000-£3000
Price Changes		xi)	Large Coronation Coach	
D Road Roller all issues	£300-£400		with King and Queen	£600-£700
N.B. 1st issue to read — all green body without a flywheel		xii)	Large Coach with just the Queen	£150-£200
(amend listing)		xiii)	Small Coronation Coach	£75-£100
ii)	Cement Mixer	xiv)	Jumbo the Elephant	£350-£450
	All issues	£100-£150	xv)	Muffin the Mule	£150-£200
iii)	Caterpillar Tractor	£150-£175			

Models of Yesteryear

After a period when the early and rarer issues appeared to have reached a price plateau, there have been some increases since 1988 and the 3rd Edition listing should be amended as follows:-

1st Issues

Y1-1	Allchin Traction Engine	
	Code 2	£75-£85
	Code 7	£400-£500
	All other codes	£75-£85
Y2-1	'B' Type London Bus	
	Code 1	£150-£200
	Code 2	£75-£95
	All other codes	£75-£85
Y3-3	'E' Class Tram Car	
	Code 3	£250-£275
Y4-1	Sentinel Steam Wagon	
	Code 1	£100-£125
Y5-1	Le Mans Bentley	
	Code 1	£120-£145
Y6-1	A.E.C. Lorry 'OSRAM LAMPS'	
	Code 2 & 3	£95-£125
Y7-1	Four Ton Leyland	
	Codes 1,2,3 & 5	£100-£150
Y8-1	Morris Cowley Bullnose	
	Codes 1 & 2	£75-£90

Y9-1	Fowler Showmans	
	Codes 2,3,4,5 & 6	£75-£90
Y10-1	Grand Prix Mercer	
	Code 1	£80-£95
	Code 6	£125-£150
	All other codes	£80-£95
Y11-1	Aveling & Porter Steam Reflex	
	All codes	£80-£95
Y12-1	Horse Drawn Bus	
	All Codes	£75-£85
Y13-1	'SANTE FE' Locomotive	
	Codes 1 & 3	£75-£85
	All other codes	£75-£95
Y14-1	Duke of Connaught	
	Code 3 and all other codes	£75-£85
Y13-1	Rolls Royce Silver Ghost	
Y16-1	Spyker Veteran Automobile	
	Codes 2,3,5,7 & 9	£25-£30
	Increase listings by 15%	

Y17- 1	Hispana Suiza		
	Codes 2-7	£6-£10	
Y23- 1	1922 AEG General		
	Code 1	£75-£100	
	Code 6 to read	£7-£10 not	£18-£24
Y24- 1	Bugatti T44		
	Codes 3 & 4	£75-£100	
Y25- 1	Renault Type 'AC' Van		
	James Neales' Codes 1 & 6	£12-£15	

Y26- 1	'CROSSLEY' Delivery Truck		
	'LOWENBRAU' Lager		
	Code 1 to read scarce not difficult		
	Code 2 delete very rare and		£90
	and substitute with NRP		
	Code 3 delete difficult and		
	substitute with very rare		£35-£50
	Code 5 delete difficult and		
	substitute with NRP		£17-£23
Y27- 1	Foden Steam Lorry		
	Codes 2 & 3		£40-£50

2nd Issues

Y1-2	1921 Model 'T' Ford	
	Code 1	£75-£100
Y4-2	Stand Mason Fire Engine	
	Codes 2 & 3	£150-£175
Y8-2	Sunbeam Motor Cycle	
	Code 1	£40-£50
	Code 4	£675-£750

Y10- 2	1926 Mercedes Benz	
	Code 1	£175-£250
Y16- 2	1928 Mercedes Benz	
	Code 55	£180-£200
	Code 6	£60-£75
	Code 12	£300-£400
Y17- 2	1918 Atkinson 'D' type Steam Wagon	
	Lake Goldsmith Code 1	£15-£20

3rd Issues

Y1-3	1936 SS Jaguar	
	Code 1	£150-£175
	Code 8	£100-£150
Y5-3	1907 Peugeot	
	Codes 5 & 7	£25-£30
Y6-3	1913 Cadillac	
	Codes 5 & 6	£75-£100
Y7-3	1912 Rolls Royce	
	Code 1,2 & 5	£20-£25
Y8-3	1914 Stutz	
	Code 4	£20-£25

Y9-3	3 ton Leyland Lorry	
	Codes 1-4	£15-£25
Y11- 3	1906 Rolls Royce Silver Shadow	
	Code 7	£15-£20
Y12- 3	1912 Ford Model 'T' Van	
	'SUNLIGHT SEIFFE' Code 1	£100-£125
Y12- 3	'IMBACH' Code 1	£10-£15
Y14- 3	Stutz Bearcat	
	Code 4	£65-£75

4th & 5th Issues

Y5-4	1927 Talbot Van	
	'LIPTONS TEA' Code 1	£16-£20
Y5-4	'NESTLES'	
	Code 2	£25-£30
	Code 3	£45-£50

Y7-4	Ford Breakdown Truck 'BARLOW'	
	Code 2	£50-£75
Y12- 5	1937 GMC Van	
	Black body grey roof	£15-£20

Code 2 Models

Y13- 3	Crossley Tender	
	'UK MATCHBOX' Code 1	£175-£225

Gift Set

Connoisseur Collection	£60-£70

Giftware Series

Prices now available as follows:-

Silver Plated Models		Gold Plated Models		Silver Plated Models		Gold Plated Models	
Y1-2	£20-£30	Y1-2	£30-£40	Y10-3	£10-£15	Y13-3	£200-£250
Y2-2	£20-£30	Y2-3	£15-£20	Y12-2	£20-£30	Y14-2	£15-£20
Y2-3	£20-£30	Y4-3	£15-£20	Y13-2	£20-£30	Y15-1	£40-£50
Y3-3	£10-£15	Y5-2	£35-£40	Y13-3	£175-£225		
Y4-3	£15-£20	Y7-2	£100-£120	Y14-2	£15-£20		
Y5-2	£25-£35	Y7-3	£15-£20	Y15-1	£15-£20		
Y6-2	£75-£95	Y10-2	£75-£95				
Y7-2	£45-£65	Y10-3	£20-£25				
Y7-3	£20-£30	Y12-2	£20-£25				
Y10-2	£30-£40	Y13-2	£20-£25				

N.B. Items detached from Giftware — please note some dealers do charge a premium for items still in their original boxes.

DINKY TOYS

Previously unlisted Set No 2 — 'Private Automobiles' sold by Lacy Scott at auction in 1989 — £1900

L — R 501 Foden 8 Wheel Diesel Wagons 1st type
502 Foden Flat Truck 1st type (Rare Colour)
503 (903) Foden Flat Truck with Tailboard 2nd type
905 Foden Chain Lorries

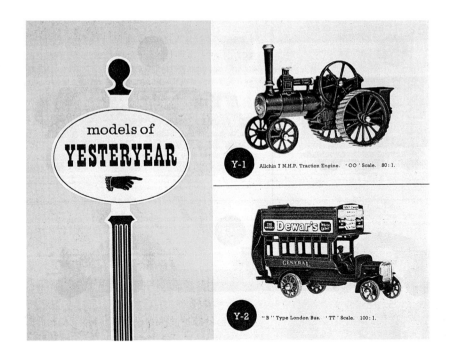

Much more about catalogues and their prices in the next main Edition

SPOT ON

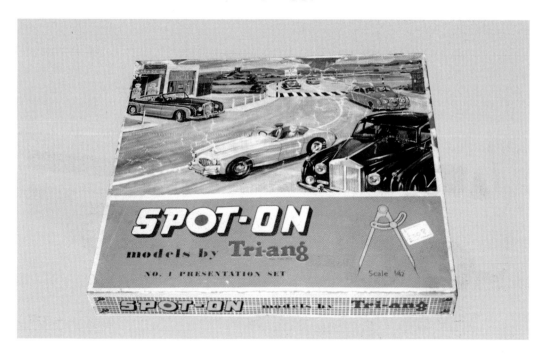

Rare No 1 Presentation Set containing 100 Ford Zodiac without lights, 101 Armstrong Siddeley, 236 Sapphire Saloon, 103 Rolls Royce Silver Wraith, 104 MGA Sports Car

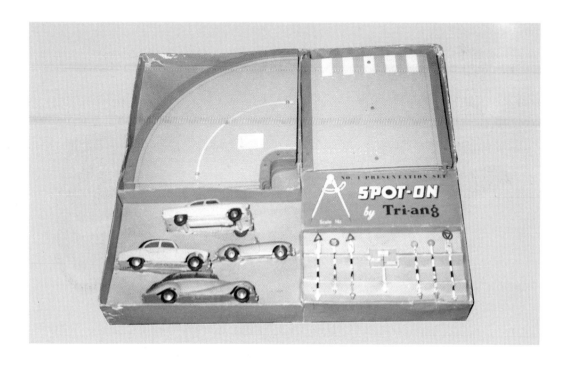

DINKY TOYS

No 944 Leyland Octopus — Rare Promotional Tanker

Picture by kind permission of Chester Toy Museum

No 935 Leyland Octopus with Chains

Both the above models form part of Mr John Kinchen's superb Dinky collection and are shown by his kind permission.

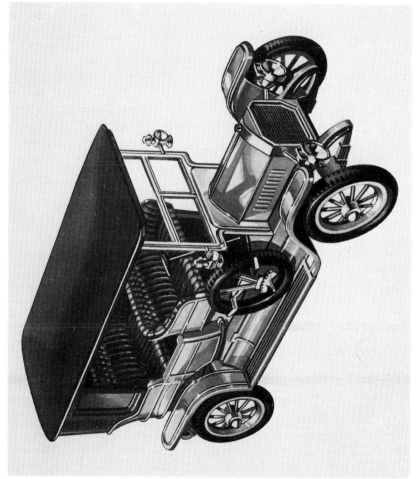

Original 'Lesney' Press Photo
Model No Y5 1907 Peugeot.

Matchbox Miniatures — New Issues and Designs

N.B. All Model Numbers are prefixed by MB

1	1989	Jaguar XJ6	White body — available from Woolworths
2	1989	S-2 Jet	Camouflage Livery (Strike Team)
3	1987	Porsche Turbo	White body, Red/blue lamps RN '14
3	1989	Porsche Turbo	Metallic blue body, bonnet emblem, yellow design
4	1989	F X 4R Taxi	Black body 'LONDON TO SYDNEY' (Australian PRM)
4	1989	1957 Chevy — Heinz	US Issue PRM
5	1989	4x4 Jeep	Camouflage Livery (Strike Team)
10	1989	Black Le Sabre	Yellow body, red skirt and RN '10
14	1988	UK (69) Corvette	Yellow body
14	1989	Articulated Tanker	Camouflage Livery (Dagger Team)
16	1989	'LAND ROVER' Ninety	Red/white body, yellow bonnet emblem
	1989	'LAND ROVER' Ninety	Camouflage Livery (Dagger Team)
17	1988	Leyland Titar	Red body, red/white/blue design 'Tour Bus
17	1989	Leyland Titar	Yellow body. 'IT'S THE REAL THING COKE' Livery
20	1988	Volvo Container Truck	Dark blue body, gold tampo 'Allders' PRM
20	1989	Volvo Container Truck	Dark blue 'COMMA OIL COMPANY' PRM
20	1989	VW Transporter	Camouflage Livery (Dagger Team)
21	1989	Chevy Breakdown	Yellow body, black hoist '24 HOURS
20	1989	Lincoln Town Car	All white body
25	1989	'AUDI QUATTRO'	Metallic grey body and design
26	1989	Volvo Tilt Truck	Blue body, yellow tilt, 'MICHELIN
	1989	Volvo Tilt Truck	Camouflage Liveries (Strike & Dagger Teams
27	1988	Jeep Cherokee	Yellow body 'BP' Dutch PRM
	1988	US Issue	Yellow body 'MR FIXER' in red
	1989	New Design	Beige body, 'HOLIDAY CLUB' Tampo
29	1989	Tractor Shovel	'THOMAS MUCOSOLVAN' logo on roof (German
33	1988	Renault II	Dark Blue, black body, silver side stripes 'Turbo
30	1989	Swamp Rat	Camouflage Livery (Strike Team
30	1989	M-Benz 280GE	White/green 'POLIZFI' no tampo on bonne
31	1989	BMW - 5 series	Dark Blue body
33	1989	Mercury Sable Wagon	All white body
34	1989	'FORD' RS2000	Blue/white body RN '2
34	1989	'FORD' RS2000	Camouflage Livery (Strike Team
36	1989	Refuse Truck	Orange Cab, blue logo, silver tippe

MB 38 Ford Models A Vans (Promotionals)

38	1988	Isle of Man 'POST OFFICE'	Red body, black roof, black island design on door
	1988	'MANX CATTERY'	Red body, black roof, 'Noble Park' design
	1988	Isle of Man 'POST OFFICE'	Red body, black roof, black island design on door
	1988	'MANX CATTERY'	Red body, black roof, 'Noble Park' design
	1988	'MERVYN WYNN'	Red body, black roof, 'Diecast Models
	1988	'W.H. SMITH & SON LTD'	Yellow body, black tampo prin
	1988	'GREENS SPONGE MIXTURE'	Green body, white tampo prin
	1988	'PMG'	Red/black body (Australian Post Office
	1988	'BIG SISTER'	No colour details (Australian
	1988	'UNIROYAL'	Black/red body, gold/red/white tampo
	1988	'NAT WEST BANK'	Blue/white/grey body 'Action Bank
	1989	'MATCHBOX SERIES'	Yellow body, black roof/chassis 'Est. 1953
	1989	'MICA CONVENTION UK'	Green/brown body 'THE BRITISH ARMY', Blue/red
			'WELCOME TO ALDERSHOT' tampo—only available to MICA member
	1989	'MICA CONVENTION USA'	Black/orange body '1989' gold tampo plus Union Jack type design
			only available to MICA members PRM
	1989	'ISLE OF MAN RACES'	White/red body, 'May 29—June 9 1989' tampo
	1989	'JORDANS'	White/black body — Mail In Offer Mode
	1989	'SHERBET FOUNTAIN'	Yellow/red body, black roof and bas
	1989	'SHERBET FOUNTAIN'	Yellow/red body, red roof and base (Woolworths only
	1989	'RIBENA'	Dark Blue body, Red/white/gold tampo
	1989	'CHEESES OF ENGLAND'	Dark blue body, yellow tampo prin
	1989	'ASDA'	Red body, black/white 'Baked Beans' tampo
	1989	'CHESTER SOUVENIR'	Available in Chester retail outlets yellow/blue body — two different
			labels, special bo

	1989	'BALTIMORE ORIOLES'	Black/orange body (USA issue)
	1989	'LION GROUP'	K.H. Norton commission red/white/blue body packed in special box
	1989	'LIGHTWATER VALLEY'	Blue/white body of tampo
	1989	'MOORLAND CENTRE'	Two tone grey body and tampo
	1989	'JUNIOR MATCHBOX CLUB'	Two tone blue body 'The Gang' etc
	1989	'COCA-COLA'	Yellow/green or yellow/red plus Coke tampo
	1989	'YORK FAIR'	Yellow/green body, green and gold tampo print
	1989	'TANDY ELECTRONICS'	Red/blue body, red/white tampo design
	1989	'CAMPERDOWN'	White/blue body, Australian Charity issue
39	1989	BMW 323c	Green body, flame design, 'BP' Dutch Prom
40	1989	Rocket Transporter	Camouflage Livery (Dagger Team)
41	1989	Porsche 935	Red body, white design, red RN '41'
43	1988	Mercedes 500 SEC	White body with silver stripes (German)
43	040	Steam Loco	Promotionals
	1989	North Yorkshire Morris	Red body
	1989	West Somerset Railway	Green body
	1989	Isle of Man Railway	'HUTCHINSON' blue body
	1989	'BLUE TRAIN'	K.H. Norton Commission — available from trade PRM
44	1988	'SKODA' 130 LR Rally	White body, red/blue tampo
46	1989	Group Racer	Two tone blue body, black aerofoil 'Savber' RN '46'
48	1988	Astra GTE	Black body, yellow/green tampo. Dutch 'BP' PRM
48	1989	Astra GTE	White body, red/blue/yellow tampo 'STP' RN '7'
51	1988	Ford LTD 'POLICE'	White body, black tampo Red 'PD-21'
52	1989	Police Launch	Camouflage Livery (Dagger Team)
53	1989	Dump Truck	Yellow body, grey tipper, red stripes
54	1988	Airport 'FOAM' Pumper	Red body, yellow tampo Red no '3'
54	1989	Ford Sierra 'XR4x4'	Yellow body, black tampo bonnet stripes
54	1989	Command Vehicle	Yellow body, red tampo and 'Foam' equipment
54	1989	Command Vehicle	Camouflage Livery (Dagger Team)
55	1989	Ford Sierra SR4i	Black body, 'Texaco' tampo RN '6'
56	1989	VW Golf GTI	Two tone metallic grey body
56	1989	Peterbilt Tanker	Camouflage Livery (Strike Team)
57	1989	Mission Helicopter	Camouflage Liveries (Strike & Dagger Teams)
58	1988	Mercedes 300L	Metallic Blue body, silver train
58	1989	Ruff Trek	White body, flame tampo (James Bond Set)
59	1989	'PORSCHE 944' Turbo	Red body, black tampo 'Credit Charge'
59	1989	'PORSCHE 944' Turbo	Black body, bonnet design
60	1988	Ford Transit Van	White body, 'Help Gt. Ormond St. Get Better' PRM
60		Ford Transit Van (Promotionals)	
	1988	'WELLA'	White body, brown/red tampo print design Germany
	1988	'WIGWAM'	White body, black/red wigwam design Germany
	1988	Ford Motor Co Issue	All green body, no tampo (Ford Box) Holland
	1988	'AUSTRALIAN POST'	Bright orange/white body 'We deliver'
	1989	'PETER COX'	K.H. Norton Commission — white body, blue/red side stripe — special box
61	1989	Peterbilt Wrecker	Camouflage Livery (Strike Team)
64		Oldsmobile Aerotech	All silver body
65	1989	Cadillac Allante	UK Issue, pink body, US Issue, silver body
65	1989	Plane Transporter	Camouflage Livery (Strike Team)
66	1988	Rolls Royce Silver Spirit	Metallic Greenish — Gold body
66	1989	Rolls Royce Silver Spirit	Metallic red body — available from Woolworths
67	1988	Ikarus Coach	White body, 'I LOVE CANARY ISLAND' PRM
68	1988	Camaro Iroc	Blue body, yellow design 'BP' Dutch PRM
68	1989	Camaro Iroc Z-28	Yellow body with blue or green tampo stripes
69	1989	Volvo 480 ES	With or without 'VOLVO' in blue on bonnet
70	1989	SP Gun	Camouflage Liveries (Strike & Dagger Teams)
70	1989	Ferrari F40	All red body, yellow emblems front and sides
72	1988	Ford Supervan	Yellow body, yellow/green design 'BP' Dutch PRM
72	1989	Dodge Delivery Truck	Red/white body 'MATCHBOX USA CONVENTION'
73	1989	Weasel	Camouflage Liveries (Strike & Dagger Teams)
73	1989	TV News Truck	Blue/grey body, red camera and boom 'MBTV' '75'
74	1989	Utility Truck	Grey body, white 'CHERRYPICKER' boom, red cas, Twin RFB
75	1988	Ferrari Testarossa	Red body, yellow emblems on bonnet and sides

Gift Sets

1988 40th Anniversary Collection Set
A recreation of 5 of the original 'Matchbox' series models including No's 1,4,5,7 and 9. For identification purposes these reissues have '1988' and 'Made in China' cast onto the body

1989 MC 10 — 10 Assorted Miniatures

Special Issues

Super GTs Miniatures

A budget range of Matchbox Cars 40 models to collect.

Super Colour Changers

Cars that change colour three times when immersed in water. 12 models to collect.

Superfast Lasers

An exciting range of 30 superfast cars with fast axles and 'high tech' metallic paint finish.

World Class Collectors Edition Series I

The Elite of Diecast Vehicles
Diecast Metal Construction Highly Detailed Trim   Detail Rubber Tyres, Metalized Windows

1. 'Porsche' 928S   Brown body
2. Lamborghini Countach   Yellow body
3. AMG 560 M-Benz   White body
4. 'Corvette' Roadster   Blue body
5. 'Porsche' 944 Turbo   Black body
6. Ferrari Testarossa   Red body
7. Ferrari 308 GTB   Red body
8. 'Porsche' 959   Silver body

Lasertronics

Battery operated range of Miniatures soon to be launched.
When pressed the models will make a siren sound and the twin roof lights flash.

MB 30H   Mercedes Benz 280GE
MB 43G   Mercedes Benz 500SEC
MB 55H   Ford Sierra XR4i
MB 72G   Ford Supervan II

Each model will be issued in three different liveries

1989 Issues

Ref No	Model	Livery	Remarks
Y3	Ford Model 'T' Tanker	Yellow/white body 'SHELL MOTOR SPIRIT'	Relivery
Y5	1927 Talbot Van	Green/white body 'LYLE'S SYRUP'	Limited Edition
Y5	1929 Leyland Titan Bus	Green/cream body, 'SOUTHDOWN'	New Model
Y8	Yorkshire Steam Wagon	Dark Blue/grey body, 'WILLIAM PRITCHARD'	Relivery and Limited Edition
Y12	GMC Van	Cream/green body 'BAXTER'S SOUP'	Relivery and Limited Edition
Y15	Preston Type Tram	Orange/cream body 'GOLDEN SHRED'	Relivery
Y12	Model 'T' Ford Van	Green/red body, 'OSRAM'	New Model
Y23	Model 'A' Van	White body, 'CHERRYBLOSSOM'	Relivery

Collectors Notes

Matchbox Models of Yesteryear — New Issues

The model listings shown in the 3rd edition were prepared by reference to the renowned "Models of Yesteryear" collectors manual "THE COLLECTION" by the kind permission of Matchbox International Ltd. "THE COLLECTION" is the Bible for all "Models of Yesteryear" collectors for it contains full colour pictures of all the models and boxes, plus a full listing of all the known model variations. Collectors will be pleased to learn that a supplement updating "THE COLLECTION" will be available in November 1989 and may be obtained from your nearest Matchbox Toys official stockist or by contacting the Matchbox Internation Collectors Association' (MICA), 42 Bridge St Row, Chester, England CH1 1NQ.

Consequently the information contained in this supplement will appear in the 4th edition of this catalogue — due to be published in the Autumn of 1990-

Late 1988 Issues

Y16/4	Scannia Half Track Bus	Yellow body and skis on front wheels. Powder blue roof, black chasis and rubber tracks. Swiss postal 'CROWN' over horn emblem 'N21'
Y21/4	1955 BMW 207 Special Limited Edition	Blue body, removable black hood, bonnet badge, number plate '681 313' detailed engine
Y6/5	1932 Mercedes L5 Lorry	White body and part rolled back canopy, grey chasis/frame red logo and wheels 'GTUTTGARTER HOFBRÄUB'
Y8/5	1917 Yorkshire Stream Lorry	Red body, grey roof, cream canopy, 'JOHNNIE WALKER'. Variation figure appears to be 'GOOSE STEPPING'
Y10/5	1931 AEC Trolley Bus 'DIDDLER'	Red/cream body, grey roof, black poles, six wheels. Route '604', 'HAMPTON COURT' 'RONUK/JEYES'
Y12/5	GMC Van	All black body, red/gold legs 'GOBLIN'. Variation black body, grey roof
Y23	A.E.C. Bus	Blue/cream body 'LIFEBUOY SOAP'. **Relivery and then withdrawn**
Y23	Mack Bulldog Tanker	Red body, 'TEXACO'. **New Model**
Y25	1910 Renault Type Van	Lilac/white body 'SUCHARD' **Relivery**
Y27	1927 Foden Steam Lorry	Purple body 'GUINNESS' **Promotional**
Y29	1919 Walker Electric Van	Green body 'HARRODS' **Packed in Harrods Green Box**

Late 1989 Issues awaited

YS-9	Leyland Cub Fire Engine	Red body, brown ladders 'WORKS FIRE ENGINE' **Special Limited Edition**
YS76	100 Tonner Scammell and Locomotive	Blue/red body 'PICKFORDS' **Special Limited Edition**

1988/89 'Passport Scheme'
The model featured was the Yorkshire Steam Wagon Y8 in 'Samuel Smith' livery and framed in an exclusive wood cabinet.

1989/90 'Passport Scheme'
The model to be featured is the 1930 Leyland Titan Y5

Corgi Toys — Revision of 3rd Edition Listings
Saloons, Estates and Sports Cars

200	Ford Consul Single Colours	£50-£60
	Two tone colours	£60-£80
200M	Ford Consul Single Colours	£60-£70
	Two tone colours	£70-£90
C200	British Leyland Mini 1000	£15-£20
201	Austin Cambridge Single Colours	£50-£60
	Two tone colours	£60-£80
201M	Austin Cambridge	£70-£90
202	Morris Cowley Single Colours	£50-£60
	Two tone colours	£60-£80
202M	Morris Cowley Single Colours	£60-£70
	Two tone colours	£70-£90
203	Vauxhall Velox including two tone	£50-£60
203M	Vauxhall Velox Single Colours	£60-£70
	Two tone colours	£70-£90
204	Rover 90 Single Colours	£50-£60
	Two tone colours	£60-£80
204M	Rover 90 Single Colours	£60-£70
	Two tone colours	£70-£90
205	Riley Pathfinder	£50-£60
205M	Riley Pathfinder	£60-£70
206	Hillman Husky Estate	£50-£60
206M	Hillman Husky Estate	£60-£70
207	Standard Vanguard	£50-£60
207M	Standard Vanguard	£60-£70
208	Jaguar 2.4 (All colours)	£50-£60
208S	Jaguar 2.4 (All colours)	£50-£60
210	Citroen DS 19	£50-£60
210S	Citroen DS 19	£50-£60
211	Studebaker Golden Hawk	£45-£60
211S	Studebaker Golden Hawk	£45-£60
211M	Studebaker Golden Hawk	£50-£60
214	Ford Thunderbird	£45-£60
214S	Ford Thunderbird	£45-£60
214M	Ford Thunderbird	£70-£80
215	Thunderbird Open Sports	£45-£60
215S	Thunderbird Open Sports	£40-£50
216	Austin A40	£40-£60
216M	Austin A40	£60-£70
224	Bentley Continental Amend listing to read Black/Silver and not Blue Silver	£40-£50
	Also add — Green and Off White version	£50-£60
225	Austin 7 Saloon	£25-£40
226	Morris Mini Minor	£25-£35
230	Mercedes Benz 220 SE coupe	
	Metallic Red, Cream, Dark Blue or Black	£30-£50
231	Triumph Herald Coupe	
	Blue/white or Gold/white	£45-£60
232	Fiat 2100	£35-£45
233	Heinkel Trojan Listing to read Orange not Yellow	£35-£70
234	Ford Consul Classic	£35-£50
235	Oldsmobile Super 88	£35-£45
236	Driving School Austin A60	£40-£50
238	Jaguar MK10	
	Metallic Blue or Cerise	£40-£50
	Metallic Green or Silver	£70-£80
239	VW 1500 Red or Cream body	£25-£35
240	Fiat 600 Jolly Light Blue	£35-£50
	Dark Metallic Blue	£50-£65

241	Chrysler Ghia L64 — Delete Green and replace with Metallic Blue or Gold	£25-£40
242	Fiat 600 Jolly	£30-£40
245	Chrysler Imperial	£40-£50
	Blue	£100-£150
247	Mercedes Benz Pullman	£25-£40
248	Chevrolet Impala	£30-£40
249	Morris Mini Cooper	£40-£50
251	Hillman Imp	£25-£40
252	Rover 2000	£30-£40
253	Mercedes Benz 220 SE	£25-£35
255	Driving School Austin A60	
	Dark blue with left hand drive	£80-£100
259	Citroen 'LE DANDY' Metallic Green	£50-£70
	Metallic Blue/white	£90-£100
262	Lincoln Continental	
	Metallic Gold body	£40-£50
	Blue body, Tan roof	£60-£70
264	Oldsmobile Toronado	£25-£35
273	Rolls Royce Silver Shadow	£40-£50
	Delete white/blue as listed under 280	
275	Rover 2000 TC	
	Metallic Green or Maroon	£35-£50
	White	£75-£90
	Metallic Lime Green	£100-£150
C280	Rolls Royce Silver Shadow	
	Whizz Wheels Issue	
	Metallic Silver and Blue body or	
	Metallic Blue body	£25-£30
281	Rover 2000 TC	£25-£35
283	'DAF CITY' Car	
	Red/Black not Brown/black	£15-£25
284	Citroen S.M. 1971-76 (not 1970-76)	
	Metallic yellow	£20-£25
	Metallic purple	£35-£40
C299	Ford Sierra 2.3 Ghia	
	Delete rare variant listing.	
	Red, Metallic Blue or Metallic Silver	£5-£10
300	Austin Healey Red or Green	£70-£80
301	Triumph TR2	£70-£80
302	MG 'A'	
	Metallic Red, Metallic Green or Cream	£70-£80
303	Mercedes Benz 300 SL Open Top	
	White/blue seats or Blue/white seats	£40-£50
304	Mercedes Benz 300 SL Hard Top	£40-£50
305	Triumph TR3	£70-£80
305S	Triumph TR3	£70-£80
306	Morris Marina 1.8 Coupe	
	Metallic Maroon or Lime Green	£20-£30
307	'E' Type Jaguar	£50-£60
316	NSU Sports Prinz	£30-£35
318	Lotus Elan	
	Metallic Blue or Green/yellow	£35-£45
N.B. Version issued with detachable chassis		
320	Ford Mustang Fastback	
	Metallic Blue or Grey	£25-£35
324	Marcos Volvo 1800 GT	£50-£60
327	MGB GT	£50-£60
334	Mini Magnifique	
	Metallic Blue or Green	£25-£35
335	Jaguar 'E' type 4.2 litre 2 + 2	£60-£70

341	Mini Marcos GT 800	£20-£25	384	Adams Probe Metallic Maroon or Blue		£10-£15
342	Lamborghini Muira		386	Bertone Barchetta		£10-£15
	Yellow or Red	£25-£40	387	Chevrolet Corvette		£20-£25
343	Pontiac Firebird	£15-£20	391	Ford Mustang		
347	Chevrolet Astra	£15-£20		This is the James Bond Version		£80-£100
372	Lancia Fulvia	£25-£35	424	Ford Zephyr Estate		£30-£40
378	MGC GT (Red/Black)	£50-£60	440	Ford Cortina Estate		£40-£50
	For yellow/black competition model see 345		485	Mini Countryman		£40-£50
	in Racing Rally section.		491	Ford Cortina Estate		£30-£40
	Orange body (Gift Set 20)	£100-£150				

Delete catalogue notes i) ii) iii) regarding models difficult to catalogue

C382	Lotus Elite 2 + 2	£10 £15

Gift Sets

1	Carrimore Transporter	£250-£350	28	Transporter and Four Cars	£200-£250
10	Camping Gift Set	£40-£50	31	Buick Boat Set	£50-£60
13	Renault 16 Film Set	£35-£40	36	Marlin Rambler Set	£50-£60
20	Golden Guinea Set	£125-£150	36	Oldsmobile Set	£50-£60
20	Transporter and Six Cars	£300-£350	48	Transporter and Six Cars	£250-£300
25	BP or Shell Garage Set	£300-£350			

Cars of the 50's Series

All issues £5-£10 with the following exceptions:-

C803	1952 Jaguar XK 120 Soft Top Sports	
Delete RARE and £100 substitute £5-£10		
C810	Ford Thunderbird, Pink	£15-£20
	Red	£10-£15

C810	1953 MG TF all issues	£10-£15
Except the cream		£15-£20
C869	MG TF Racing Car	£10-£15
Gift Sets — 100 years set		£15-£20
Jaguar Set		£20-£25

Auction Price Results
Lacy Scott's Bury St. Edmunds Auctions 1989

Gift Set 38 Mini Rover and Citreon (E)		£120
202	Morris Cowley (M) boxed	£50
334	Mini Magnifique (M) boxed	£40
224	Bentley Continental (M) boxed	£35
259	Citreon 'LE DANDY' (M) boxed	£75
203	Vauxhall Velox (M) box damaged	£48
335	'E' Type Jaguar (M) unboxed	£45
320	Ford Mustang	£28
238	Jaguar MK X (Pale Blue) (M) boxed	£36

No 1 Set Car Transporter Empty Box		£30
236	A60 Motor School (M) boxed	£22
261	James Bond's Aston Martin (M) boxed	£70
305	Triumph TR3 (M) boxed	£50
Gift Set 48 Car Transporter and Six Cars		
	Box damaged, models (M)	£150
Gift Set 20 A Tri Deck Car Transporter with 6 whizz		
	wheels cars, box damaged Models (M)	£110
Gift Set 48 May 89 (M)	*Phillips*	£200

Collectors Notes

Original Corgi Toys Press Photo
No. 335 The Jaguar 2+2 E-Type Coupe

Racing, Rally and Speed Cars

	Models C100 to 139/4 all	£3-£5	317	Monte Carlo 1964 Mini Cooper S	£60-£70
150	Vauxhall Racing Car	£40-£45	318	Monte Carlo 1965 Mini Cooper S	£60-£70
150S	Vauxhall Racing Car	£40-£50	319	Lotus Elan Hard Top	£35-£45
150	Surtees TS9 Formula 1	£15-£20	321	Monte Carlo Mini Cooper S 1965-66	£50-£60
151	Lotus X1 Racing Car			1966 only Racing No '2' with signatures	
151S	Lotus X1 Racing Car			on roof	£80-£90
	Delete White, colours are Turquoise		322	Monte Carlo Rover 2000	£50-£60
	Blue, or Silver/grey	£40-£50		1967 only International Rally finish	
152	BRM Racing Car	£40-£50		white/black body RN 21	£70-£80
152S	BRM Racing Car		323	Monte Carlo Citroen DS 19	£60-£70
C152	Ferrari 312 B2 (Not £75!)	£15-£20	325	Ford Mustang	£25-£30
153	Bluebird Record Car	£40-£50	328	Monte Carlo Hillman Imp	£35-£45
153S	Bluebird Record Car		330	Porsche Carrera 6	£20-£25
153	1972-74 Team Surtees TS9B	£15-£20	333	1967 (not 1966 as shown)	
154	Ferrari Formula 1	£20-£25		Mini Cooper S	£70-£80
155	Lotus Climax Racing Car	£20-£25		Model also found in GS 48	
C155	'SHADOW' F1 Racing Car	£15-£20	337	Chevrolet Stock Car	£15-£25
156	Cooper Maserati Racing Car	£20-£25	339	Monte Carlo 1967 Mini Cooper S	£60-£70
	Models C156 to C170 all	£15-£20	340	Monte-Carlo Sunbeam Imp	£40-£50
190	'JOHN PLAYERS SPECIAL' Lotus	£25-£35	344	Ferrari Dino Sports	£25-£30
191	'TEXACO MARLBORO' Mclaren	£25-£35	345	MGC GT (not MGB GT as shown)	
C201	Mini 1000 Team 'CORGI'	£15-£20		Yellow/Black	£50-£60
227	Mini Cooper Rally	£50-£60	371	Porsche Carrera 6	£15-£20
256	VW Safari Rally	£40-£50	376	Corvette Stock Car	£15-£20
282	Mini Cooper Rally	£25-£35	385	Porsche 917	£15-£20
302	Hillman Hunter Rally	£35-£45	394	Datsun 240 Z	£15-£25
304S	Mercedes Benz 300 SL Hard Top	£50-£60	396	Datsun 240 Z	£15-£25
305	Mini Marcos GT 850	£25-£35		Porsche-Audi 917-10	£10-£15
C308	Mini Cooper 'S'	£25-£30		Models 399-422 inclusive	£5-£10
309	Aston Martin DB4	£35-£45	423	Brooklyn Ford Escort	£10-£15
312	Jaguar 'E' Type	£45-£50	424	Ford Mustang	£10-£15
314	Ferrari Berlinetta 250LM	£20-£25	426	'HEPOLITE' Rover	£10-£15

Gift Sets

5	Racing Car Set	£100-£125	C26	F1 Racing Car Set	£15-£20
6	Racing Car Set	£45-£60	29	Ferrari Racing Set	£20-£25
12	Grand Prix Racing Set 1969-71		C29	Lotus Racing Set	£15-£20
	Contains 155,156,330 and 490 plus trailer		32	Lotus Racing Team Set	£70-£80
	and equipment. Later version with 158		38	Monte-Carlo Rally Set	£200-£250
	and 159 is the same price	£100-£125	45	All winners set	£200-£300
15	Silverstone Set	£300-£350	46	All winners set	£125-£175
16	Ecurie Ecosse Transporter and Four Cars	£150-£200	C48/1	Racing Set	£5-£10
17	Ferrari and Land Rover	£60-£70			
25	Racing Car and Tender Set	£40-£50			

Major Pack

	Ecurie Ecosse Transporter	£70-£80

Auction Price Results

Lacy Scott, Bury St. Edmunds 1989 Auctions

319	Lotus Elan (2) boxed		£40
GS38	Monte-Carlo Rally Set (E) box poor		£130
GS46	All winners (M)	*(Phillips 5/89)*	£200
GS No 5	Racing Car Set (G) box damaged		£48
GS37	Lotus Racing Team (M)	*(Phillips 5/89)*	£95

Small Commercial Vehicles and Vans

403	Bedford 12 cwt Van 'DAILY EXPRESS'	£65-£75
403	Bedford 12 cwt Van 'KLG PLUGS'	£80-£100
404	Bedford Dormobile	£35-£50
404M	Bedford Dormobile	£45-£40
407	Smiths Karrier Mobile Grocery Shop	£45-£60
408	Bedford 12 cwt Van 'A.A.'	£65-£80
411	Karrier Bantam Van 'LUCOZADE'	£65-£80
413	Karrier Bantam Mobile Butchers Shop	£45-£60
421	Bedford 12 cwt Van 'EVENING NEWS'	£75-£90
422	Bedford 12 cwt Van 'CORGI TOYS'	£85-£100
426	Karrier Bantam Circus Booking Office	£90-£100
C426	Chevrolet Booking Office Van	£20-£25
428	Karrier Bantam Ice Cream Van	£60-£70
C431	Vanatic Chevvy Van	£10-£15
433	Volkswagon Deliver Van	£45-£60
435	Karrier Bantam Dairy Produce	£60-£70
C437	'COCA-COLA' Chevvy Van	£15-£20
441	Volkswagon Van 'TOBLERONE'	£60-£70
443	Plymouth Suburban Mail	£45-£50

447	Ford Thames 'WALLS ICE CREAM'	£50-£60
450	Austin Mini Van	£40-£50
452	Commer Dropside Lorry	£60-£70
453	Commer Refrigerated Van	£65-£75
454	Commer Platform Lorry	£45-£60
455	Karrier Bantam 2 tonner	£45-£60
456	ERF 449 Dropside Lorry	£50-£60
457	ERF 449 Platform Lorry	£50-£60
	Blue/yellow version	£50-£60
459	ERF 449 Van 'MOORHOUSE'	£125-£150
462	Commer 'CO-OP' Van	£70-£80
462	Commer 'HAMMONDS' Van	£90-£100
471	Karrier Bantam Van 'JOE'S DINER'	£45-£50
	(New Entry) Belgian issue 'POTATES FRITES'	£75-£100
474	Musical 'WALLS' Ice Cream	£50-£70
479	Commer Mobile Camera Van	£45-£60
484	Dodge Livestock Transporter	£20-£25

Gift Sets

11	ERF Dropside (Cement/Planks)	£70-£80
21	ERF Dropside (Milk Churn Load)	£80-£90
24	Commer Constructor Set	£60-£70
1151	Scammell 'CO-OP' Set	£250-£300

Escort Vans

The following models now have a premium:-

503	'TELEVERKET'	£15-£20
504	'JOHN LEWIS'	£10-£15
514	'CHUBB'	£10-£15
?	'WAITROSE'	£10-£15
C543	'TELEVERKET'	£10-£15
C557	'FIRE SALVAGE' (Gift Set Only)	£10-£15
C566	'WILTSHIRE FIRES (Gift Set Only)	£10-£15
C562	'GAMLEYS'	£10-£15
C496	'MANCHESTER EVENING NEWS'	£10-£15
C564	'TELEVERKET'	£15-£20
C577	'PLESSEY'	£15-£20
C578	'BEATTIES'	£15-£20
	All other issues	£5-£10

Ford Transit Vans

	UK Issues	£3-£5
656/12	'KTAS' Danish	£6-£8
656/16	'BUNDESPOST' German	£6-£8

Mercedes Vans

All issues	£4-£8

Collectors Notes

Large Commercial Trucks and Tankers
Major Packs and Large Size Models

Bedford Trucks

)0	'S' Type Carrimore Lowloader	
	Red cab, blue loader	£60-£70
	Yellow cab, blue loader	£70-£80
)1	'S' Type Carrimore Car Transporter	
	Red cab, blue transporter	£50-£60
	Blue cab, yellow transporter	£70-£80
)4	'S' Type Carrimore Machinery Carrier	
	Red cab, silver semi trailer	£50-£60
	Blue cab, silver semi trailer	£60-£70
)4	'TK' Type Horse Transporter	£30-£40
l0	'S' Type 'MOBIL' Tanker	£125-£150
29	'S' Type 'MILK' Tanker	£150-£175
31	'TK' Type Machinery Lowloader	£60-£70
32	'TK' Type Lowloader	£60-£70
l8	'TK' Type Car Transporter	£45-£60
40	1965-67 (not 66-67)	
	'TK' 'MOBILGAS' Tanker	£150-£175
41	1965-67 (not 66-67)	
	'TK' 'MILK' Tanker	£150-£175

Berliot Commercial Trucks

l05	Racehorse Transporter	£25-£30
	'UNITED STATES LINES'	£20-£25

) Ford Commercial Trucks

)8	'MICHELIN'	£5-£20
)9	'MICHELIN'	£20-£25

1137	'EXPRESS SERVICES'	£35-£45
1138	'CORGI CARS'	£50-£60
1157	'ESSO'	£20-£25
1158	'EXXON'	£20-£25
1159	Car Transporter	£25-£30
1160	'GULF'	£20-£25
1161	'ARAL'	£25-£30
1169	'GUINESS'	£20-£25
1170	Car Transporter	£15-£20
1191	'FORD QUALITY'	£10-£15
?	'BALLANTINES'	£20-£25
?	'KAYS'	£5-£10

iv) Mack Commercial Trucks

1100	'TRANSCONTINENTAL'	£35-£40
1106	'A.C.L.' Container Truck	£35-£40
1152	Mack 'ESSO' Tanker	£35-£40

v) Scammell Commercial Trucks

1146	Tri Deck Car Transporter	£60-£70
1147	'FERRYMASTERS'	£50-£60
1151	CO-OP Promotional	£150-£250
	(Boxed in Brown cardboard)	

Agricultural Models

Massey Ferguson '65' Tractor	£40-£50	
Massey Ferguson Tractor with shovel	£45-£50	
Fordson Half Track Tractor	£100-£125	
Fordson Major Tractor	£45-£50	
Massey Ferguson Tractor with stook	£50 £60	
Beast Carrier	£15-£20	
Fordson Power Major Tractor	£45-£50	
Ford Tipper Trailer	£10-£15	
Conveyor on Jeep	£25-£35	
Massey Ferguson '65' Tractor	£45-£50	
Ford Super Major Tractor	£45-£50	
Massey Ferguson Tractor & Shovel	£45-£50	
Ford '5000' Tractor & Towbar	£45-£50	
Massey Ferguson Tractor & Saw	£45-£50	
Ford '5000' Tractor & Scoop	£45-£50	
2 Rice's Pony Trailer		
Tractor & Beast Carrier	£50-£60	
Land Rover and Pony Trailer	£25-£35	
Country Farm Set	£35-£45	
Agricultural Set	£125-£150	
Tractor and Trailer Set	£60-£70	
Combine Tractor Trailer Set	£90-£100	

9	Trailer, Tractor, Shovel Set	
	contains 62 and 69 (not 66)	£60-£70
13	Fordson Tractor and Plough Set	£60-£70
15	Land Rover and Horse Box	£20-£35
18	Ford Tractor and Plough Set	£60-£70
22	Agricultural Set	£200-£250
	Contains 51,53 with Fork,	
	55,566,101,406,1111, 1487, 1490 and 3	
	figures	
29	Massey Ferguson Tractor and Trailer	£60-£70
32	Tractor Shovel & Trailer Set	£50-£60
33	Tractor and Beast Carrier	£50-£60
C42	1978-79 Agricultural Set	£35-£40
	Contains C55 & C56, Silo & Elevator	
C43	Auger and Silo Set	£15-£20
47	Ford Tractor and Conveyor Set	£70-£80
C47	Pony Club Set	£15-£25
1111	Massey Fergusson Combine	
	with metal tines	£50-£60
	with plastic tines	£40-£50
C112	1978-79 David Brown Combine (CJJ)	
	coupled to Danish J.F. Combine	£25-£30
1129	Beaufort Double Horse Box	£15-£20

Ambulance, Fire, Police and Rescue Vehicles

209	Riley Police Car	£50-£60
213	Jaguar Fire Service Car	£50-£60
213S	Jaguar Fire Service Car	
223	Chevrolet State Police Car	£40-£50
237	Oldsmobile Sheriff's Car	£40-£50
C236	Chevrolet Caprice Police Car	£15-£20
C332	Opel Doctors Car	£15-£20
C339	Rover 3500 Police Car	£10-£15
333	— 361 inclusive	£5-£10
373	VW 1200 Police Car	£20-£25
402	Ford Cortina Police Car	£15-£20
405	Bedford Fire Tender	£70-£80
405M	Bedford Fire Tender	£80-£90
C406	Mercedes Ambulance	£10-£15
412	Bedford 12 cwt Ambulance	£50-£60
C412	Mercedes Police Car	£10-£15
414	Jaguar XJ12C 'COASTGUARD'	£15-£20
416	R.A.C. Land Rover Both issues	£50-£60
C416	Buick Police Car	£10-£15
419	Ford Zephyr Motorway	£40-£50
421	Land Rover (Forest Warden)	£20-£25
422	Riot Police Wagon	£10-£15
423	Bedford Fire Tender	£70-£80
437	Superior Cadillac Ambulance	£35-£45
439	Chevrolet Fire Chiefs Car	£40-£45
448	Police Mini Van	£45-£50
461	Range Rover Police Vehicle	£10-£15
463	Commer Ambulance Cream or White	£45-£50
464	Commer 15 cwt Police Van	£45-£60
	German issue (Green)	£100-£150
481	Chevrolet Police Car	£40-£45
482	Chevrolet Fire Chiefs Car	£45-£50
482	Range Rover Ambulance	£15-£20
492	Volkswagon Police Car	£25-£30
506	Sunbeam Imp Police Car	£35-£45
509	Porsche Targa Police Car	£20-£25
513	Citroen ID 19 'ALPINE RESCUE'	£40-£50
541	— 656 all issues	£5-£8
700	Motorway Ambulance	£10-£15
703	Hi Speed Fire Engine	£10-£15
921	Hughes 'POLICE RESCUE'	£8-£10
924	Air Sea Rescue Helicopter	£8-£10
927	Surf Rescue Helicopter	£10-£15

Major Packs

C1001	HCB Angus Firestreak	£30-£40
1103	Airport Crash Truck	
	Airport Fire Brigade	£30-£40
	New York Airport	£20-£30
1120	Dennis Fire Engine	£5-£8
1126	Simon Snorkel	£20-£25
1127	Simon Snorkel	£35-£45
C1143	'AMERICAN LA FRANCE' Fire Engine	
	Early Picture Box	£40-£50
	Later Window Box	£25-£30
1185	Mack Fire Engine	£5-£10

Gift Sets

18	Emergency Gift Set	£25-£35
C19	Emergency Gift Set	£20-£25
C20	Emergency Gift Set	£25-£30
C35	'CHOPPER SQUAD' Surf Boat	£25-£35
C44	Police Land Rover & Horse Box	£25-£35
C45	Canadian Mounties Land Rover/ Horsebox	£45-£50

Export Sets

All		£10-£15

Taxis

221	Chevrolet Impala Cab	£40-£50
C327	Chevrolet Caprice Taxi	£15-£20
388	Mercedes 190 Taxi	£20-£25
418	Austin Taxi	£5-£10
430	Ford Bermuda Taxi	£45-£50
480	Chevrolet Impala Taxi	£40-£45

Gift Sets

11	London 'OUTSPAN'	£60-£70
C11	London 'B.T.A.'	£25-£30
35	London 'CORGI TOYS'	£70-£80
2	Wiltshire Fire Brigade	£35-£40
	Dennis Fire Engine (1120) plus Escort Van	
C1/2	London Scene	
	'LONDON STANDARD'	£15-£20
C2	Fire Set	£15-£20
C/8/2	Police Set	£15-£20
C19	Emergency Police Set	£15-£20
C/27	Emergency Set	£15-£20

Military and R.A.F. Models

350	Thunderbird Missile & Trolley	£25-£35
351	RAF Land Rover	£35-£45
352	RAF Vanguard Staff Car	£40-£50
353	Decca Radar Scanner	£15-£20
354	Commer Military Ambulance	£40-£50
355	Commer 'MILITARY POLICE' Van	£50-£60
356	Commer 'PERSONNEL CARRIER'	£60-£70
357	Land Rover Weapons Carrier	£60-£70
358	1961 Oldsmobile Staff Car	£65-£75
359	Commer Army 'FIELD KITCHEN'	£60-£70
414	Bedford Military Ambulance	£40-£50
500	US Army Land Rover	£80-£100
C900— C908	inclusive all issues	£10-£15
C909	British Tractor Gun & Trailer	£20-£30
C910	Bell Army Helicopter	£10-£15
C923	Sikorsky Sky Crane Helicopter	£10-£15

Major and Large Size Models

106	Karrier Decca Radar Van	£50-£60
108	Bristol Bloodhound Guided Missile	£65-£75
109	Guided Missile on Loading Trolley	£65-£75
112	Corporal Guided Missile on Ramp	£65-£75
113	Corporal Missile and Erector Vehicle	£90-£100
115	Bristol Ferranti Bloodhound Missile	£40-£50
116	Launch Ramp for 1115	£25-£35
118	International 6x6 Army Truck	£70-£80
124	Corporal Missile and Launch Ramp	£25-£35
133	Troop Transporter	£80-£90
1134	'US ARMY' Fuel Tanker	£150-£200
1135	'US ARMY' Transporter	£150-£200

Military Gift Sets

3	Ramp with Thunderbird Missile	£80-£90
4	Bloodhound Missile Set	£125-£130
6	Guided Missile Set	£300-£350
9	Corporal Missile Set	£175-£200
10	Centurion Tank Transporter Set	£25-£30
17	Military Set	£30-£40

Collectors Notes

104	Dolphin Cabin Cruiser	£15-£20
C107	Batboat on Trailer	£20-£25
	Whizz wheels	£15-£20
201	The Saints Volvo P1800	
	Red label with white 'SAINT' design	£35-£45
N.B. Also available in GS48		
258	The Saints Volvo P1800	
	White label with black 'SAINT' design	£35-£45
C259	Penguinmobile	£10-£15
C260	Superman Police Car	£15-£20
261	James Bonds DB5 Aston Martin	£75-£90
C261 — 265	All issues	£15-£20
266	Chitty Chitty Bang Bang	£125-£150
267	Batmobile	
	1st Issue Picture Box plus Bat design on wheels	£125-£150
	2nd Issue Window Box no design on wheels	£50-£60
	3rd Issue Whizz Wheels	£25-£35
	4th Issue No Robin Figure	£20-£25
268	Green Hornet	£125-£150
C268	Batbike	£20-£25
C269	James Bonds Lotus Espirit	£35-£40
270	James Bonds Aston Martin	£40-£50
	Rare spoked wheels early version	£60-£75
C271	James Bonds Aston Martin	£25-£35
C272	James Bonds Citroen 2CV	£10-£15
277	The Monkeemobile	£90-£100
C278	Dan Dare Car Delete Listing (never issued)	
C290	Kojak Buick	£15-£20
C292	Starsky and Hutch Ford Torino	£20-£25
	Delete reference to reissue in 1986	
C298	Magnum's PI Ferrari	£20-£25
C320	The Saints Jaguar	£15-£25
336	James Bond's Toyota 2000	£85-£100
C342	The 'PROFESSIONALS' Ford Capri	£20-£25
C348	Vegas Thunderbird	£15-£20
395	Firebug	£15-£20
426	Circus Booking Office	£90-£100
C426	Circus Booking Office Jean Pinder	£20-£25
C434	'CHARLIES ANGELS'	£10-£15
C435	'SUPERVAN'	£10-£15
C436	'SPIDERMAN'	£10-£15
436	Citroen Safari ID 19	£40-£50
472	Land Rover 'VOTE FOR CORGI'	£50-£60
475	Citroen Safari Winter Sports	£60-£65
475	Citroen Safari 'CORGI SKI CLUB'	£45-£50
486	'KENNEL CLUB TRUCK'	£40-£45
487	'CHIPPERFIELDS'	
	Land Rover with clown & chimpanzee	£65-£75

497	Man from U.N.C.L.E.	£70-£8
	Rare white version	£200-£25
499	Citroen 1968 'GRENOBLE' Olympics	£60-£7
503	Giraffe Transporter (Land Rover)	£50-£6
510	Citroen DS19 Team Managers	£45-£5
511	Circus Poodles Track 1970-71 Chevrolet	£150-£17
513	Citroen Safari Alpine Rescue	£60-£7
607	Elephant Cage Plastic kit with elephant	£20-£2
C647	Buck Rogers Starfighter	£15-£2
C648	NASA Spaceshuttle	£10-£1
C649	James Bonds Space Shuttle	£25-£3
801	Noddy's Car	
	2 figures	£70-£8
	3 Figures	£80-£9
802	Popeye's Paddle Wagon	£150-£20
803	Beatles Submarine	£150-£20
805	Hardy Boys Rolls Royce	£70-£8
806	Lunar Bug	£50-£6
807	Magic Roundabout Car	£100-£15
807	Dougalls Car 1971-74	£70-£8
808	Basil Brush's Car	£60-£7
809	Dick Dastardly's Car	£40-£5
811	James Bond's Moon Buggy	£100-£15
851	Magic Roundabout Train	£85-£10
852	Musical Carousel	£90-£10
853	Magic Playground	£250-£30
859	Mr McHenrys Trike	£45-£5
860 — 868	Magic Roundabout Figures	£10-£2
C926	Stromberg Helicopter	£20-£2
C925	Batcopter	£20-£2
C928	Spidercopter	£15-£2
C929	'DAILY PLANET' Jetcopter	£10-£1
C930	Drax Helicopter	£20-£2

Major Packs

1119	H.D.L. Hovercraft		£25-£3
1121	Circus Crane Truck		£60-£7
1123	Circus Cage 'CHIPPERFIELDS'		£35-£5
1130	Circus Horse Transporter		£150-£17
1139	Scammell Handyman Circus		£150-£17
1144	Circus Crane and Cage		£15-£2
C1163	Circus Cannon Truck		£20-£2
C1164	Dolphinarium Truck		£25-£3
2030 — 2032		Kermit	£20-£2
		Kozzy	£15-£2
		Animal	£10-£1

Add 15-20% to all models not listed

Corgitronics and Corgimatics

C1001	HCB Angus Firestreak	£30-£40	C1009	MG Maestro 1600	£15-£
	All other prices largely unchanged				

Original Corgi Toys Press Photo
Major Pack 1139 Scammell Handyman Circus Transporter

Gift Sets

C3	Batmobile and Batboat	
	1st issue	£65-£80
	2nd issue whizz wheels	£40-£50
7	Daktari Gift Set	£60-£70
8	'LIONS OF LONGLEAT'	£50-£80
12	Circus Gift Set	£85-£100
14	Giant Daktari Set	£100-£125
19	Chipperfield Circus Cage	£75-£80
21	Circus Gift Set 1970-72	£350-£450
C21	Superman Set	£40-£50
C22	James Bond Set	£125-£150

25	'CHIPPERFIELDS' Circus Set	£300-£350
C23	Spiderman Set	£50-£60
C30	Circus Set	£25-£30
C31	Safari Land Rover and Trailer	£35-£40
C36	Tarzan Set	£70-£80
40	The Avengers Set	£225-£250
C40	Batmans Gift Set	£80-£90
C40	Batmans Set (2 models)	£40-£50
C41	Silver Jubilee Set	£15-£20
C48	Circus Set Jean Pinder	£60-£70

Roadmaking Vehicles, Cranes and Hoists

54	Delete listing see Farm and Garden	
109	'PENNYBURN' Trailer	£10-£15
403	Thwaites Skip Dumper	£10-£15
406	Mercedes Unimog	£15-£20
409	Unimog Dumper	£5-£20
C409	'ALLIS CHALMERS' Forklift	£15-£20
458	ERF Earth Dumper	£30-£40
459	Raygo Rascal Dumper	£20-£25
460	ERF Cement Tipper	£30-£40
483	Dodge Tipper Truck	£25-£30
494	Bedford Tipper	£25-£30

1102	EUCLID TC12 TRC	£45-£50
C1102	'BERLIET' Bottom Dumper	£25-£30
1103	'EUCLID' Crawler	£45-£50
1107	'EUCLID' with Dozer	£45-£50
1110	J.C.B. Crawler	£15-£20
C1113	'HYSTER' Handler	£15-£20
1128	'PRIESTMAN' Cub Shovel	£25-£30
1145	Unimog Goose Dumper	£15-£20
1153	Priestman Crane	£45-£50
1154	Priestman Crane Truck	£45-£50
C1155	'SKYSCRAPER' Tower Crane	£20-£25
1156	Volvo Concrete Mixer	£20-£25

Major Packs

C1101	Mobile Crane	£20-£25

Miscellaneous

406	Land Rover Pick Up	£45-£50
49	Forward Control Jeep	£20-£25
C415	Mazda Camper	£20-£25
417	Land Rover	£35-£40
C419	Covered Jeep C35	£10-£15
420	Ford Thames 'AIRBORNE' Caravan	£30-£50
431	Volkswagon Pick Up	£45-£50
434	Volkswagon Kombi	£40-£45
438	Land Rover	£20-£25
465	Commer Pick Up Truck	£30-£35
470	Forward Control Jeep	£25-£30
477	Land Rover Breakdown	£20-£30
478	Jeep Tower Wagon	£15-£20
C490	Volkswagon Breakdown	£30-£35
C493	Mazda 1600 Pick Up	£10-£15
702	Breakdown Truck	£5-£10

Major Models

1116	Refuse Collector	£10-£15
1117	Streetsweeper	£10-£15
1142	'HOLMES WRECKER'	£40-£50
1144	Berliet Wrecker Recovery	£35-£40
1100	Unimog with snow plough	£20-£25

Gift Sets

17	Delete reference see Racing Cars Gift Sets	
19	'CORGI FLYING CLUB' (1973-77)	£20-£30
28	Mazda Dinghy Set	£20-£30
C49	'CORGI FLYING CLUB' (1978-80)	£20-£25
64	Jeep 150 and Conveyor	£35-£40
C/20/2 & C/21/2 'A.A.' & 'R.A.C.' Sets		**£15-£20**

Corgi Classics Price Review

The following listings refer solely to those models which by reason of their collectability have attracted a premium. The models shown have been extracted from the full listing given in the 3rd edition. In addition new issues which have already attracted a premium have also been included.

1 A.E.C. Forward Control Cabover

597/3	'L.M.S. EXPRESS PARCELS'	£40-£50
C945/10	'BP OIL' (promotional)	£15-£20

2 Bedford 'OB' Series

Single Decker Coaches

0949/1	'NORFOLKS'	1st Type	£40-£50
		2nd Type	£40-£50
C949/2	'ROYAL BLUE'		
	1st type with skirt small letters		£50-£60
	2nd type as 1st with large letters		£40-£50
	3rd type without skirt large letters		£30-£40
C949/3	'BLUEBIRD' Amend to read white body, blue roof		£15-£20
C949/6	'SOUTHDOWN'		£50-£60
C949/10	'HIGHLAND'		£20-£30
C949/11	'EAST YORKSHIRE' 5000 certificated		£25-£30
C949/13	'HANTS & SUSSEX'		
	1st type creamy pink flash (2500)		£25-£30
	2nd type white flash (1000)		£25-£30
	'SOUTH MIDLAND'		£15-£20
	'WALLIS ARNOLD' (5000)		£15-£20
	'SOUTHERN VECTIS' 5000 Certificates (Nov 89)		£15-£20

Pantechnicons

C953/1	'PICKFORDS'	£60-£70
C953/2	'WARING & GILLOW'	£30-£40
C953/3	'FRASERS OF IPSWICH'	£30-£40
C953/4	'STEINWAY & SONS'	£15-£20
C953/7	'CAMP HOPSON'	£15-£20
D953/9	'STYLO'	£15-£20

Box Vans

C822/4	'SOLIDOX'	£20-£25
D822/5	'MILLERS' hidden 'BAKING POWDER' logo variant	£30-£40

Ford Model 'T' Vehicles

Vans

C874	'CORGI COLLECTOR CLUB' 2nd anniversary	£15-£20
C966	'FORDS 75th Anniversary' (with certificate)	£15-£20

Morris 1000 Vehicles

Vans

C957/1	'ROYAL MAIL' plastic base	£15-£20
C957/3	'CORGI COLLECTOR CLUB 3rd ANNIVERSARY'	£15-£20
C958	'POST OFFICE TELEPHONES' Plastic base	£15-£20
C957/7	'MAC FISHERIES'	£15-£20

Cars

C701/1	'BRITISH SCHOOL OF MOTORING'	£5-£10
C702/2	Dark Blue	£5-£10
C703/1	'POLICE' Panda Car	
	1st type (7000) thick quarterlights etc	£15-£20
	2nd type (2000) thin quarterlights etc	£30-£40

N.B. For full details see new issue section

1926 Renault
Canvas Backed Truck

C925	'GERVAIS DANONE'	£10-£15

N.B. BP Promotional Models please note that the unsold balance of the models used namely i) A.E.C. Forward Control Cabover 'POTTERS ASTHMA CURE' ii) A.E.C. Tanker 'BP PETROLEUM' and iii) Thorneycroft Double Decker Bus 'SCHWEPPES' were released to the trade in the winter of 1988.

1929 Thorneycroft Vehicles
Box Vans

821	'BUHRMANN'	£15-£20
828	'GAMLEYS'	£15-£20
C830	'W & R JACOB'	£30-£40
C831	'HUNTLEY & PALMERS'	£10-£15
C822	'CORGI COLLECTOR CLUB 1ST ANNIVERSARY'	£15-£20
	1st type wrong address	£25-£35
C834	'LYONS SWISS ROLLS' (with certificate)	£50-£60
C840	'ALLENBURYS'	£20-£25
C841	'PEER FREANS'	£15-£20
C842	'CARTER PATERSON'	£15-£20
C843	'EDDERSHAWS'	£15-£20
C846	'IND COOPE'	£10-£15
C847	'KEILLERS'	£10-£15
C848	'NEWS OF THE WORLD'	£10-£15
C849	'GOODYEAR'	£30-£40
C853	'M.A. RAPPORT'	£10-£15
C907	'H.P. SAUCE'	£10-£15
C910	'SMALL & PARKES'	£10-£15
C911	'PERSIL'	£10-£15
C924	'SAFEWAY'	£10-£15
C926	'DOUBLE DIAMOND'	£10-£15
C931	'STEPNEY TYRES'	£20-£30
968	'RADIO STEINER'	£35-£45

Box Vans with Billboards

C859/3	'ARNOTTS'	£25-£35
C859/5	'GRATTANS'	£10-£15
C929	'GAMLEY'S'	£10-£15

Beer Trucks with barrel load

C821/1	'HEIDELBERGER'	£10-£15

Canvas Backed Trucks

C827	G.W.R.	
	1st type without GWR logo or sides	£10-£15
	2nd type with GWR logo on sides	£20-£30
C836	L.M.S.	£20-£30
C837	'SOUTHERN RAILWAY'	£15-£20
C838	'L.N.E.R.'	£20-£30

Double Decker Bus

C888	'GRANTS MORELLO CHERRY BRANDY'	£25-£30

Thorneycroft Body & Renault Bonnet

C902	'ROYAL MAIL'	£50-£60

Gift Sets

C49 & C50	Transport of the 30's Sets	£15-£20
C68 & C69	Transport of the 30's Sets	£15-£20
C88	Military Gift Set	£20-£25
C89	60 Years of Transport	£25-£35
C90	Model 'T' Ford Utility Set	£15-£20

Corgi Classics — Original Issues

9001	1927 Bentley	£30-£35	9021	1910 38 h.p. Daimler	£35-£45
9002	1927 Bentley	£35-£40	9031	1910 Renault 12/16	£25-£35
9004	'WORLD OF WOOSTER' Bentley	£60-£70	9032	1910 Renault 12/16	£25-£35
9011	1915 Model 'T' Ford	£30-£35	9041	1912 Rolls Royce Silver Shadow	£25-£35
9012	1915 Model 'T' Ford	£30-£35		Re-released original classics all	£5-£10
9013	1915 Model 'T' Ford	£30-£35			

Original Corgi Toys Press Photo
No. C469 London Routemaster Bus

Routemaster Double Deckers

C469	'CADBURY'S DOUBLE DECKER'		£10-£15
C469	'SELFRIDGES'		£15-£20
C469	'LEEDS PERMANENT'		£15-£20
C469	'BLACKPOOL ILLUMINATIONS'		£35-£45
C469	'REDGATES'		£45-£50
C469	'LONDON TRANSPORT GOLDEN JUBILEE'		£45-£55
C469	'BLACKPOOL PLEASURE BEACH'		£45-£55
C469	'BLACKPOOL PLEASURE BEACH (Open Top)		£45-£55
C469	'NORBROOK'	Blue	£20-£25
		Red	£30-£35
C469	'JOLLY GIANT'	Yellow/green	£10-£15
		Red	£15-£20
C469	'DION DION DION'		
	1st issue		£15-£20
	2nd (Incorrect label)		£20-£25
C469	'MANCHESTER LIONS CLUB'		£25-£35
C469	'THE NEW CORGI COMPANY'		£25-£30
C469	'ESSEX ORGAN STUDIOS'		£13-£18
C469	'COWES STAMP & MODEL SHOP'		£15-£20

C469	'FARNHAM MALTINGS'		£20-£25
C470	'DISNEYLAND'		£15-£20
C471	'SEE MORE LONDON'		£15-£20
C471	'WOOLWORTHS SILVER JUBILEE'		£20-£25
C523	'BRITISH DIECAST MODEL TOYS CATALOGUE'		
	1st white letters		£10-£15
	2nd gold letters		£20-£25
C633	'HOSPITAL RADIO'		£10-£15

N.B. Increase the prices shown for the other Routemasters listed in the 3rd edition by 15%

Corgi Coaches

1120	'MIDLAND RED COACH'		£55-£65
C1168	'GREYHOUND'		£10-£15
C1168	'MOTORWAY EXPRESS'		£10-£15
C1168	'EURO EXPRESS'		£10-£15
C1168	'ROVER BUS'	Blue	£10-£15
		Cream	£15-£20

Collectors Notes

Corgi Toys — New Standard Issues

Saloon, Estates and Sports Cars

C522	1988	Range Rover	All Brown body '40th Anniversary'
C435/7	1989	Volvo Saloon	Mid blue body
C440/3	1988	Porsche 944	All black body
C386/6	1988	Mercedes 2.3/16	Dark blue body
C330/2	1989	Mini 'ROSE'	Pink/white body
C330/3	1989	Mini 'RACING'	Dark Green/white body, gold logo
C330/4	1989	Mini — 'FLAME'	Red/white body
C330/5	1989	Mini — 'SKY'	White/blue body

Racing, Rally and Speed Cars

C299/3	1988	Sierra Rally	Black body, Red 'TEXACO' design
C353/4	1988	BMW 325i Rally	White body with Blue/Red bands 'CASTROL'
C386/4	1988	Mercedes Rally	White body with yellow bands 'BURLINGTON'
C399/5	1988	Peugeot Team Car	Yellow body, red/blue design 'VATENAN'
C441/1	1988	'PORSCHE' 944	White body, Union Jack designs
C325/1	1988	Jaguar XJR 9	White body, 'CASTROL' 'RN 60'
C144/1	1988	'JAGUAR' XJR 9	White body, 'CASTROL' 'RN 66'

Ford Escort 55 Vans

C496/17	1988	'FORD'	White body, blue stripe, brown interiro
C496/18	1988	'GAS'	Blue/white body 'BRITISH GAS' logo
C496/20	1988	'UNIGATE'	Red/white body 'FRESH MILK' logo
C496/9	1988	'BRITISH TELECOM'	Yellow body, no opening doors type 3

Buses, Minibuses, Coaches, Metrobus

AEC Regent Double Decker Bus (Classic Series Models)

C599/4	1988	'GLASGOW'	Green and Brown body, 'CROWN WALLPAPERS'
C599/5	1988	'RHONDDA'	Red body, Yellow design panel 'PREMIUM BONDS'
C599/6	1989	'MORECAMBE'	Mid Green body, white bands, 'HEYSHAM'
C599/7	1989	'BRADFORD'	Blue body, white bands and design panel

Metro Bus

C675/4	1988	'BEATTIES'	Red body, black mudguards, yellow design '25'
C675/6	1989	'YORKSHIRE'	Red/white body, yellow/red design
C695/9	1988	'HITACHI'	Dark Green body, red/black striped design

Ford Transit Minibus

C676/1	1988	'BLUEBIRD'	Dark blue/white body 'MIDLAND SCOTTISH' Livery
C675/5	1988	'ROYAL MAIL'	Red body, yellow roof, 'POST BUS' (5000) PRM
C676/7	1989	'BRITISH AIRWAYS'	Grey/blue body with red side flash
C676/6	1989	'CHASERIDER'	Red/yellow body '25' 'MINIBUS'

Routemaster Double Decker Buses

C469/8	1988	'JACOBS'	Red body, pale orange/black design panel
	1989	'THE GREAT BOOK OF CORGI 1956-1983' Special Issue	

Available only to purchasers of the above book
Resplendent in Corgi blue/yellow livery with above logo

Ambulance, Fire, Police and Rescue Vehicles

C674/1	1988	Ford TSV Breakdown	Yellow body, white stripe, black hoist 'AA'
C674/2	1988	Ford TSV Breakdown	White body, Red/blue band 'RAC'
C597/3	1989	Range Rover	All white body, yellow flash POLICE
C438/3	1989	W Mercia Rover	All white body, yellow/blue flashes POLICE

Large Commercial Trucks and Tankers

Scammell Commercial Trucks

C1246/8	1989	'FAO SCHWARZ'	All white body, rocking horse designs (US Market)

Seddon Atkinson Trucks

C1238/5	1988	'SILENTNIGHT'	White body, black chassis 'HIPPO' design
C1238/6	1989	'DATAPOST'	Red body, black chassis 'ROYAL MAIL'
C1238/9	1989	'CADBURYS'	White body with purple side panels

Volvo Trucks and Tankers

C1222/4	1989	Car Transporter	Yellow/grey cars and decks
C1231/27	1989	'SAS CARGO'	White body, black chassis & logo (Swedish Market)
C1265/2	1989	'TEXACO'	White cab and tank, Grey chassis
C1231/29	1989	'INTERMARCHE'	Orange/white body and cab (French Export)
C1238/3	1989	'GULF' Tanker	White/blue cab, Black/orange tank

Vans

Mercedes 207 D Vans

C576/10	1989	'C.R. SMITH'	White/blue body 'DOUBLE GLAZING'

Ford Transit Van

C656/21	1988	'LYNX'	Black body, red design 'EXPRESS DELIVERY'

Gift Sets — Standard Issues

Tourist Sets with different background inserts to boxes

C30	Tower Bridge Set	
C469	'EVENING STANDARD'	(425/1) Black Taxi
C31	Piccadilly Set	Same as C30 plus Sierra Police Car (358)
C32	Big Ben Set	Same as C30 plus Concorde Model
C344	Tower of London	As C31 plus Concorde Model, figures and C438/3 Rover 'POLICE' Car

Export Models

Taxis

388/2	1988	Mercedes (Denmark)	White body with green design 'TAXI'
C435/6	1988	Volvo (Denmark)	Blue/red body, opening bonnet 'TAXI'
C435/6	1988	Volvo (France)	Red body, blue 'TAXI' sign on roof

Saloons

C435/5	1988	Volvo 740	Maroon body (Sweden)
C57	1988	Volvo 740/Caravan	Red body only available with set (Sweden)

Ambulance, Fire, Police and Rescue Vehicles

C358/2	1989	Sierra (Norway)	White body 'POLITI' in blue, 2 blue FLL
C361/1	1988	Volvo Car (Sweden)	White body, POLIS In blue, twin or single RFB
C361/2	1988	Volvo Car (Denmark)	White body, 'POLITI' in blue, FLLB
C386/3	1988	Mercedes Car (Germany)	Green/white body, POLIZEI, twin RFB
C542	1989	Mercedes Bonna Ambulance	Red/white body, red cross, twin RFB 'RODEKORS HJELPEKORPS (Norway)
C597	1989	'SOS 101' Range Rover	White body, central red flash, Belgium

Gift Sets

C11/1	1989	'NOTRUF' Set (Swiss)	Red Range Rover 'FEVERWEHR' Mercedes Bonna Ambulance (white) plus 454 'POLIZEI' Car
C19/6	1989	'AMBULANCE' Set	Ford Transit 'AMBULANSSI' white/red, plus black 'POLIISI' Car (Finland)
C93	1988	Police Set (Sweden)	C361/1 Volvo plus helicopter in white/red 'POLIS'

Ford Transit Vans

C656/18	1988	Falck (Denmark)	Red body 'SERVICE VOGN'

Ford Transit Minibus

C676/4	1988	Falck (Denmark)	White body, red band, 'SYGETRANSPORT'

Plaxton Coach

?	1988	'POHJOLAN LIKENNE'	All white body, Zig Zag side design (Finland)

Collectors Notes

Corgi Classics — New Issues

N.B. Where some models are already being sold with a premium these are shown

Box Vans, Trucks, Tankers, Vans, Cars, Buses, Tramlines
AEC Forward Control Cabovers
Box Vans

C897/7	1988	'MARS'	Dark Brown/cream/red body (3200)
D897/9	1988	'INTERNATIONAL'	Blue green/yellow body, black chassis
D897/11	1988	'JOHN BARKER'	Dark Brown body, white cab roof
D897/12	1989	'ROYAL MAIL'	Red body, black cab roof and chassis, gold logo

Production quantities of models already listed: C897/1 (4500), C897/2 (5900), C897/3 (3700), C897/4 (7400), C897/5 (8400), C897/6 (9800), C987/10 (21000)

Tankers

C945/5	1988	'SOMERLITE OIL'	Light blue body, white cab roof (3500)
C945/6	1989	'REDLINE GLICO'	Red body, black cab roof and chassis
Part			
D9/1 Set	1989	'SHELL MEX'	Green/red body, 'SURE OF SHELL' logo MOM

Production quantities for models already listed: C945/1 (4500), C945/2 (5200), C945/3 (9100), C945/4 (7400)

Bedford C.A. Vans

D981/1	1989	'PICKFORDS'	Dark blue body, white logo 'JUL 118'
981/2	1989	'CAMBRIAN NEWS'	White/black body, 'ABERYSTWYTH' 'TCC 189'
981/3	1989	'A.A.'	Yellow/black body, 'ROAD SERVICE' '122 GMY'

Bedford Dormobile

D982/1	1989	'Dormobile'	Cream/blue body, silver trim VTM 48
D982/2	1989	'Dormobile'	Red/blue body, silver trim

Bedford 'OB' Series
Single Decker Coach

C949/8	1988	'SOUTH MIDLANDS'	Red/white body, black wings, gold logo (4900)	
C949/9	1988	'PREMIER'	Two tone blue body (5000)	
C949/10	1988	'HIGHLAND'	Cream/maroon body Kay Mom (3100)	
C949/11	1988	'EAST YORKSHIRE'	Cream body, blue side flash (3000 certificates)	£25-£30
C949/12	1989	'CLASSIC'	Light blue body, red wings & side flash	
C949/13	1989	'HANTS & SUSSEX'	Maroon body, red roof and wings	
			1st issue creamy pink flash (2500 approx)	£25-£30
			2nd issue Rerun with white flash (1500 approx)	£25-£30
C949/14	1989	'WALLACE ARNOLD'	White body, red roof, wings and flash (5000 certificate)	£15-£20
C949/15	1989	'MACBRAYNES'	Red body, green roof, white windows/flash	
	1989	'SOUTHERN VECTIS'	Tilling green, cream flash, black wings (5000 certificates)	£15-£20

Production quantities for models already listed:- C949/1 (3000), C949/1 2nd (5800), C949/2 2nd (550), C949/3 (10,000), C949/4 (970), C949/5 (9500), C949/6 (4400), C949/7 (5000)

Bedford 'OB' Series continued
Box Vans

C822/2	1988	'TATE & LYLE'	White/red/dark blue body, 'PURE BRITISH' (4000)	
C822/3	1988	'GILLETTE'	Two tone green body, black wings, red hus (4800)	
D822/4	1989	'CARTER PATERSON'	Green/red body 'SOLIDAX TOOTHPASTE'	
D822/5	1989	'MILLERS'	Cream/green body 'BAKING POWDER'	
			Variant 'BAKING POWDER' logo hidden behind cab	£30-£40
D822/7	1989	'CADBURYS'	Green body, red roof and wings, white logo	
D822/8	1989	'MALTESERS'	Brown cab, red/white box, red wings and wheels	

Production quantity for models already listed C822/1 (6700)

Pantechnicons

C953/7	1988	'CAMP HOPSON'	Cream/brown body, green/orange removals design (4300)
C953/9	1989	'STYLO'	Blue/black body, red logo 'STEPOUT'
C953/10	1989	'WEETABIX'	Yellow/brown body, 'MORE THAN A BREAKFAST FOOD'
C953/2	1989	'BISHOPS MOVE'	Yellow/white/black body 'REMOVAL/STORAGE'

Production quantities for those models already listed:- C953/1 (10400), C953/2 (3800), C953/3 (4500), C953/4 (8200), C953/5 (9100), C953/6 (8400)

Fordson 5 cwt Van (Ford Popular)
A superb new model with diecast body and base and featuring plastic wheels, rubber types detailed base, spare wheel on nearside door, number plates front and rear, and theatre grille.

D980	1989	'CORGI CLUB 89'	Dark Blue body, black wings and wheels
D980/1	1989	'S.A. PEACOCK'	Bright green/black body, red wheels 'HAULAGE'
D980/2	1989	'FULLERS'	Light blue/red body 'THE RADIO PEOPLE' 'HKM75U'
D980/3	1989	'LUTON MOTOR CO'	Sea Green/dark brown body 'Tractor Division'
			— variation with lighter brown front wings
D23/1	1989	'FRASER COOK LTD'	Purple body, black wings (Grattans MOM)
D23/1	1989	'LEWIS EAST LTD'	All black body (Grattans MOM)
D23/2	1989	'SIGNSMITHZ'	Light blue body, black wings (Grattan MOM)
D72/1	1989	'BOWYERS'	Dark brown body, white logo 'WILTSHIRE SAUSAGE'
D72/1	1989	'COLMANS MUSTARD'	Yellow body, black wings, red wheels
D74/1	1989	'PICKFORDS'	Dark blue body, white roof, red wheels (Kays MOM)
D980/8	1989	'C. PEARSON'	Green/black body, 'QUALITY CARPETS' 'KNM 562'

Mack Trucks

C906/8	1988	'BOVRIL'	Cream body, red billboards/wings, black cab (4300)

Production quantities of models already listed as follows:-

C906/1 (12500) including (2700) US issues with lighter hub shade   C906/2 (9800), C906/3 (9100), C906/4 (11,600), C905/5 (11600) C906/6 (9100), C906/7 (4600), C906/10 (4600)

Ford Model 'T' Vans

C865	1989	'LYONS TEA'	French Issue blue body black roof
C865/11	1989	'STEIFF'	Brown/black body with billboards (UK issue) (5300)

C865 (18500), C865/1 (7000), C805/2 (5800), C805/3 (8400), C865/4 C865/5 'TWINNINGS' (7100), C879 (5000), C874 (4100), C877 (5000), C965 gold logo (5000), white logo (3000)

Morris 'J' Van Expected Early 1990 Issues

D983/1	1989	'P.O. TELEPHONES'	Green/black body, white logo, gold crown
D983/2	1989	'ROYAL MAIL'	Red/black body gold logo and crown 'E II R'

Morris Minor 1000 Vans

Production quantities for models already listed:-
C957/1 Royal Mail (10,000 metal and 10,000 plastic base), C957/2 (7800), C957/3 (5800 1st wheels and 1700 2nd wheels), C957/6 Foyles (6700), C958 (10,000 metal & 10,000 Plastic base)

C957/5	1989	'MICHELIN'	Yellow body 'MAKE SURE ITS A MICHELIN' in blue
C957/7	1988	'MACFISHERIES'	Mid blue body with white wavy line design (3700)
C957/8	1989	'GRATTANS'	Green body (Grattans MOM Set) (5000)
C957/9	1989	'TELEGRAPH & ARGOS'	Yellow body (Grattans MOM Set) (5000)
C957/10	1989	'MITCHELLS'	Cream/blue body (Grattans MOM Set) (5000)
C957/11	1989	'APPLEYARDS'	Pale green body, yellow blade, 'NUFFIELD TRACTOR'
D957/12	1989	'D. MORGAN'	All blue body, red logo 'FRIARS ENTRY OXFORD'
D957/13	1989	'KIMBERLEY CLARK'	Mid blue bodfy 'HI-DRI' paper towels
D13/1	1989	'POLICE VAN'	All black body, white logo, 'GATESHEAD INCIDENT' (GSM)
D13/1	1989	'POLICE VAN'	All white body, blue logo, 'DOG SECTION' (GSM)
D72/1	1989	'RINGSTON'S TEA'	Yellow/black body, gold logo (GSM)
D72/1	1989	'FRY'S COCOA'	Cream/brown body, cream logo (GSM)

1926 Renault
Box Vans

C824		'MARCEL GARDET'	All blue body (21500)

Production quantities for models already listed:- C824/2 (9000), C824/3 (3800), C902 (2500), C917 (12000), C925 (13000) C823/1, C823/1 (22500)

Beer Truck

D889/1	1989	'STELLA ARTOIS'	Red/white body, black cab and chassis

Thorneycroft Box Van with Billboards

C839/9	1988	'ASDA'	Blue body, yellow coachlines, food design (9700)
C859/10	1988	'BATCHELORS PEAS'	Green/cream/blue body 'PICK OF CROP'
C859/7	1989	'LEDA SALT'	Two tone grey body, black billboards (3900)
C859/11	1988	'LEA & PERRINS'	Orange body, black roof and wings (7300)
C859/13	1989	'MCDOUGALLS'	Two tone brown body, red wings

Production quantities for models already listed but no figue shown:- C821 (2500), C821/1 (8200), C833 (9500), C845 (10000), C859 (1400), C859/1 (6700), C859/2 (6400), C859/3 (8200), C859/4 (10,000), C859/5 (5200), C911 (5000), C913 (1300), C94 (15000), C915 (12000), C924 (3000), C929 (5000), C931 (3500), C932 (5000), C933 (3000), C968 (5000 including 1500 Swiss Export)

Thorneycroft Beer Truck with Barrel Load

CV867/4	1988	'CARLSBERG'	Green/white body 'Green design' (5700)

Production quantities for models already listed:- C867 (17000), C867/1 (7900), C867/2 (6800), C867/3 (6700), C882 (5000), C883 (5000)

Thorneycroft Double Decker Bus

C858/11	1988	'GREAT EASTERN R'WAY'	White/red body, red logo certificated (3900)

Production quantities for models already listed:- C858 (25000), C858/1 (14800), C858/2 (8100), C858/3 (7400), C858/4 (4500), C858/5 (8900), C858/6 (9600), C858/7 (8300), C858/8 MILITARY BUS (4600), C858/9 'BAXTERS' (31000), C858/10 'SCHWEPPES' (24,500), C884 (4800), C858 (5300), C888 (5900), C975 (6300)

Tramlines

Single Decker Tramways

D990/3	1989	'DERBY CORPORATION'	Green main body, white roof, driver
D990/4	1989	'WOLVERHAMPTON'	Green/white body, red/yellow logo, driver and conductor

Production quantities for models already listed:- C990/1 (7200), C990/2 (6300)

Double Decker Tramways — Open Top

D991/2	1988	'BLACKPOOL CORPORATION'	White/green body with three different saloon end variants i) Green ends ii) White ends iii) white & green ends (7800)
D991/3	1989	'BATH ELECTRIC'	Beige/blue body and platforms

Production quantities for models already listed:- C991/1 (6300)

Closed Top Tramways — Double Deckers

Production quantities for models already listed:- C992/1 (6100), C992/2 (7600), C992/3 (8700)

C992/4	1988	'BLACKPOOL'	White/green body (Kays Mail Order) (3100)
C992/5	1988	'BRADFORD'	Cream body, blue roof/platforms, Orange chassis (5000)
D992/6	1989	'SOUTHAMPTON'	Red/white body 'BLACK & WHITE WHISKY' logo
D992/7	1989	'BIRMINGHAM'	Cream/dark blue body 'BIRMINGHAM POST'

Fully Closed Double Deck Tramways

D993/1	1989	'PORTSMOUTH'	Dark red/white body 'BRICKWOODS ALES & STOUT'
D993/2	1989	'DOVER'	Green/white body 'HURTLEY PRESERVES'

Open Top Tramways

D991/4	1989	'BOURNEMOUTH'	Brown/yellow body, beige interior 'COUNTRY GATES'
D991/5	1989	'BURTON & ASHBY'	White/brown body 'HOLIDAYS ISLE OF MAN'

Cars

Ford Cortina — Lotus 1963/64

D708/1	1989	White body, lime green stripe, silver trim 'KVV 33D'
D708/2	1989	Black body

N.B. New issues awaited in 1989 in Red and Aqua Blue Liveries

Ford Popular Saloon 1935-1959

C701/1	1988	Grey blue body and wheels, red interior 'DKG 180'
C701/3	1989	Black body and wheels, beige interior 'HOC 236'
C701/5	1989	Fawn body and interior 'HPY 15'

Ford Zephyr Saloon 1956-62

D710/1	1989	All black body, red interior, silver trim '110 LAC'
D710/2	1989	All blue body, black interior, silver trim '8445 TW'
D710/3	1989	Monaco Red (Regency grey expected late 89)

Ford Zodiac Saloon 1956-62

D709/1	1989	Maroon/grey body, beige interior, silver trim DCH/DWS
D709/2	1989	Dark blue/light blue body, beige interior 'WKY 256'
D709/3	1989	Yellow/white body
D709/4	1989	Red/white body

MGA — Hard Top and MGA — Open Top

N.B. New castings of each model expected late 89

Jaguar — MKII Saloon 1959

C700/1	1988	Red body, silver trim, 'Jaguar' emblem on bonnet (9200)
C700/3	1988	Black body, issued with certificate (6000)
C706/1	1988	'POLICE' all black body (7000)
D700/4	1989	Metallic fawn body, beige interior 'KYU 418D'
D700/5	1988	All green body, beige interior, 'NUB 254 E'
D700/6	1989	Metallic blue body, beige interior, '928 JTT'
D700/7	1989	Metallic grey body, red interior '659 DYT'

Morris Minor Saloon 1948-1969

C701/1	1988	Black body, 'BRITISH SCHOOL OF MOTORING' (9600)	£5-£10
C702/2	1988	Dark blue body, silver trim DGV '929 H' (11900)	£5-£10
D702/4	1989	Lilac body, grey bumper, silver trim '797 CUY'	
D702/5	1989	Maroon body, black interior 'RBR 96J' (few issued)	
D702/6	1989	Almond green body, black interior 'DUJ 748Cb	
D703/1	1989	'POLICE' Panda Car, Pale blue body, white doors 'PE5 645 J'	
		1st type — small separate wheel hobs	
		— thin end of roof sign attached to roof	
		(7000) No front windows detail — ie no mirror or wipers thick	
		quarterlights	£15-£20
		2nd type — non separate wheel hubs (larger than 1st type)	
		— detailed windscreen and wipers	
		(2400) Thin quarter lights	
		— thick end of roof sign attached to roof	£30-£40

U.S. Models

C528/2	1989	Chevy Bed Air	Pale blue/white body, silver fin LHD
C810/2	1989	Ford Thunderbird	Black body, white striped fin, LHD/WUT

D/71	1989	'ROYAL MAIL' Set	Bedford 'OB' Box Van — Red/black body
			Morris Minor Van — all red body
C91	1989	Morris Van	Grattans Mail Order (5000)
		Triple Set	a Green body 'GRATTAN'
			b Cream/brown body 'MITCHELLS'
			c Yellow body 'TELEGRAPH & ARGUS'
D9/1	1989	'SHELL' Twin Set	Grattans Mail Order — Limited Edition
		1910-1940	a Thorneycroft Box Van 'SHELL OIL & SHELL PETROL'
			b A.E.C. Cabover Tanker 'YOU CAN BE SURE OF SHELL'
D13/1	1989	Morris 1000 Van	Model a — Black body 'GATESHEAD POLICE INCIDENT VAN'
		'POLICE' Set (2)	b — white body 'DOG SECTION'
D17/1	1989	Bedford 'OB' Series	Grattans Mail Order — Limited Edition
		'SHELL' Twin Set	a Box Van — yellow/red body
		1950-1960	b Pantechnicon — white/yellow body
D23/1	1989	Ford Popular	Grattans Mail Order
		Triple Van Set	a Purple/black body, 'FRASER COOK LTD'
			b Black body 'LEWIS EAST LTD'
			c Light blue/black body 'SIGNSMITH'
D71/1	1989	Model 'T' Ford	Kays Mail Order — Limited Edition
		Four Model Set	a Tanker — Blue body 'SOMERLITE'
			b Tanker — Red body 'TEXACO'
			c Van — Red/brown 'AI SAUCE'
			d Van — White/black body 'APS MEDICINE'

Production quantities for Gift Sets already listed:- C49 (8900), C50 (5000), C68 (5000), C69 (10000), C88 (6000), C89 (5000), C90 (10000)

D72/1	1989	Morris Minor &	Kays Mail Order — Limited Edition
		Ford Popular Van Set	a Morris Van 'RINGTON'S TEA'
			b Morris Van 'FRY'S COCOA & CHOCOLATE'
			c Ford Popular Van — 'BOWYERS WILTSHIRE SAUSAGES'
			d Ford Popular Van — 'COLMANS MUSTARD'
D74/1	1989	'PICKFORDS' Set	Kays Mail Order — Limited Edition
			a 'OB' Series Pantechnicon — Blue/white body
			b Morris Minor Van — Blue/white body
			c Ford Popular Van — Blue/white body
D75/1	1989	3 piece 'POLICE' Set	Kays Mail Order — Limited Edition
			a Jaguar Mark II — White body
			b Morris Minor Panda — Blue/white body
			c Ford Zephyr — Black body
D16/1	1989	Rallying with Ford	Limited Edition — Certificates
			a Ford Zodiac — yellow/white RN '21'
			b Ford Zephyr — Monaco Red, RN '29'
			c Ford Popular — Pale green, No RN
D14/1	1989	Bedford CA Van Set	Limited Edition
			a Yellow body 'DANDY', b Blue body 'BEANO'

Collectors Notes

BUDGIE TOYS   Price Review

The prices listed in the 3rd edition have been proved to be somewhat low and the main changes are as follows:-

202	Refrigeration Truck	£20-£25
204	Volkswagon Pick Up	£20-£25
206	Leyland Hippo Truck	£30-£35
208	R.A.F. Personnel Carrier	£60-£70
210	British Army Personnel Carrier	£60-£70
212	U.S. Army Personnel Carrier	£75-£100
214	Thorneycroft Crane	£25-£35
216	Renault Long Wheelbase	£30-£40
218	Seddon 'AA' Jumbo Traffic	£75-£85
220	Leyland Hippo Cattle Truck	£25-£35
222	US Tank Transporter	NGPP
224	Tank Locomotives	£15-£20
226	Foden Dump Truck	£15-£20
228	Commer 'COCA COLA' Van	£50-£60
230	Seddon Timber Transporter	£30-£40
282	Seddon Cable Drum Transporter	£45-£55
234	Tractor Transporter	NGPP
236	Routemaster Bus	£15-£20
238	Scammel Scarab 'CADBURYS'	£55-£65
	(original issue) 'RAILFREIGHT'	£55-£65
240	Scammell Scarab with tilt	£35-£45
242	Euclid Tipper	£25-£35
244	(Delete Austin) Morris Breakdown Lorry	£30-£35
246	Wolseley 'POLICE' Car (original issue)	£35-£45
248	Wells Fargo Stage Coach with four horses	
	Red Stage, 3 white, 1 brown horse	£100-£150
250	Number used in connection with packs of small scale models	
252	Austin Container Truck	£55-£65
254	A.E.C. Fire Escape (Merryweather)	£35-£45
256	'ESSO' Pluto Tanker	£75-£95
258	Daimler Ambulance	£55-£75
260	Ruston - Bucyrus Excavator (1962 only)	NGPP
262	Racing Motorcycles 1962 only	
	Black rider, red helmet, blue M/Bike	NGPP
264	Racing Motorcycle and Sidecar (1962 only)	
	Black rider and passenger, red machine and helmet	NGPP
268	Express Delivery Motorcycle 1962-64	
	Black rider, white helmet, blue M/Cycle, red side car	NGPP

268	'A.A.' Land Rover	£45-£55
270	Leyland Hippo Tanker	£45-£55
272	Supercar (1962 only)	£125-£150
274	Refuse Truck (Ford Thames)	£25-£30
276	Bedford Long Wheelbase Tipper	£25-£35
278	R.A.C. Land Rover	£45-£55
280	A.E.C. Refuelling Tanker	£125-£150
282	Euclid Scraper	£10-£15
284	Euclid Crawler Tractor (never issued)	
286	Euclid Bulldozer (never issued)	
288	8 Wheel Albion Carrier	£30-£40
290	Bedford Ice Cream Van	£65-£75
292	Albion Milk Tankers	
	Red/white or Blue/white versions	£65-£75
294	Bedford TK Horse Box	
	2 brown horses, Luton box	£30-£40
296	Motorway Express Coach	£65-£75
298	Alvis Salamander Tender	£45-£55
300	Lewin Sweepmaster	£45-£55
302	Commer Lift Truck 'B.O.A.C.'	£45-£55
304	Bedford TK Glass Truck	£45-£55
306	Fiat Tractor with shovel	£40-£50
308	Seddon Low Loader 'PITT'	£40-£45
310	Leyland Cement Mixer	£35-£45
312	Bedford 'SUPER TIPMASTERS'	£40-£45
314	Fiat Truck with shovel	£35-£45
316	Overhead Tower Wagon	£35-£45
318	Euclid Mammoth Damper	£35-£45
322	Scammell Routeman	£40-£50
324	Douglas Duo Tipper	£30-£40
326	Scammell Highwayman	£35-£45
452	A.A. Motorcycle Patrol	
	1st type black sidecar mudguard (1958-63)	£45-£55
	2nd type yellow sidecar mudguard (1963-66)	£45-£55
454	R.A.C. Motor Cycle Patrol	
	1st type black sidecar mudguard (1958-63)	£45-£55
	2nd type blue sidecar mudguard (1963-66)	£45-£55
456	Solo Motor Cycle Patrol (All issues)	£25-£35

Gift Set 5. (New Entry) contains 256, 238 (Rail Freight), 308, 312   £125-£175

Morestone Models

Leyland Scammell 17 ton	£35-£45		Daimler Ambulance	£55-£65
International A170	£35-£45		Personnel Carrier	£60-£70
Guy Arab Double Deck Bus	£75-£85		Albion 'MILK' Wagon	£65-£75
Guy Otter 'PICKFORDS' Pantechnican	£75-£85		Caravan	£100-£150
Foden Petrol Tanker	£75-£85		Stage Coach	£100-£150
Foden Long Distance Wagon	£75-£85		A.A. & R.A.C. M/Cycle Patrols	£45-£55
Foden Dump Truck	£30-£40		A.A. Land Rover	£45-£55
Foden 14 ton Chain Lorry	£75-£85			

EFE Models Exclusive First Editions Limited

Scale 1:76 0:0 Gauge

Exclusive First Editions is an entirely new range of diecast models with an exclusive difference — a constant scale.

Research amongst enthusiasts and collectors established that there was a significant need not being met by existing manufacturers.

That need was for a range of commercial vehicles produced to scale. Of course, having decided to fulfil that market requirement, only one scale was appropriate — "00".

In selecting '00', exclusive First Editions is able to provide a wide range of models that will appeal to both vehicle and railway enthusiasts alike.

For the first time, '00' scale train layouts will be made to look even more authentic with this range of faithfully produced commercial replicas.

The models included in the range represent some of the most interesting and significant commercial vehicles to be seen on the roads during the 50's and 60's.

Issues as at 1st October 1989

A.E.C. Regent

Double Decker Bus

Diecast body, detailed plastic base and wings 'A.E.C. REGENT', plastic hubs, rubber tyres with 'EFE LTD'. Front and rear and side destination boards, windows, mud brown plastic interior, silver/black plastic grille, cream plastic desk divider.

	Issue Date	Livery	Details
10101	1989	'DURACELL' 'LONDON TRANSPORT'	Red/black body No 38 VICTORIA 1st registration number RT 981 Rare 2nd registration number RT 206
10102	1989	'BUXTED' 'GREENLINE'	Dark green body, lighter green base/wings and base, 'RAILWAY RELIEF ONLY'
	1989	'BEATTIES' 'LONDON COUNTRY'	Mid green, red/blue labels No.314 2 Waters Garage

Commissioned Models

	Issue Date	Livery	Details
C101005	1989	'50 YEARS OF RT BUS' 1939-89	a Red body, 'LONDON TRANSPORT' in gold (1008) b Green body 'LONDON TRANSPORT' in gold (1008)
?	1989	'ATKINSON'S ALES' 'COVENTRY TRANSPORT'	Maroon body
C101004	1989	'STAR CONSTRUCTION' 'LONDON TRANSPORT'	Red body, dark cream spacer, extra set of labels (1008 cert) (Hedingham)

Open Top Bus

Construction and components as for the Double Decker Bus, without the roof and top deck windows.

	Issue Date	Livery	Details
10201	1989	'BEACHY HEAD' 'EASTBOURNE CORPORATION'	White body, bright blue base/wings, No. 6 'PRINCES PARK'
10202	1989	'COLMANS MUSTARD' 'GREAT YARMOUTH TRANSPORT'	Dark blue body and base 'SEAFRONT SERVICE CAISTER'

Commissioned Model Expected Late 1989 early 1990 'COLMANS MUSTARD' 'LONDON TRANSPORT' Red body (Stretton Models)

EFE Forthcoming New Issues and Expected Release Dates

A.E.C. Regent Vehicles
Double Decker Bus

C101001	OCT/NOV 1989	'PEARL ASSURANCE' 'GREENLINE'	Lincoln Green body (2016) Commissioned by Vectis Models
C101002	OCT/NOV 1989	'SMITHS BEEF' 'BIRMINGHAM'	Blue/cream body (1512) Commissioned by Stretton Models
C101007	OCT/NOV 1989	'EVENING DESPATCH' 'MIDLAND RED'	Cherry red body (1512) Commissioned by Stretton Models
C101009	OCT/NOV 1989	'DULUX' 'GLASGOW CORPORATION'	Yellow/green body Commissioned by Vectis Models (1008)
C101010	OCT/NOV 1989	'PAIGNTON 200' 'DEVON GENERAL'	Maroon body Commissioned by Stretton Models

Open Top Bus

C102001	OCT/NOV 1989	'SEE THE ISLAND' 'SOUTHERN VECTIS'	Cream body 'FROM THE TOP OF A BUS' Commissioned by Vectis (1008)

A.E.C. Mammoth Major Vehicles

Box Vans

October 1989	'START RITE'	Red cab and chassis and logo, cream box
October 1989	'LONDON CARRIERS'	Green body, white logo
November 1989	'CROFT ORIGINAL'	Brown cab and logo, white box
November 1989	'PICKFORDS'	Dark blue body, black chassis, white logo

Flatbeds

October 1989	'BLUE CIRCLE'	Yellow body and wheels, blue logo
October 1989	'FURLONG BROS'	Cream body and wheels, brown logo
January 1990	'BATH & PORTLAND'	Blue body and wheels, white logo
January 1990	'LONDON BRICK'	Red body and wheels, black logo

Dropside

October 1989	'BRITISH STEEL'	Blue body and wheels, white logo
October 1989	'WHITBREAD BREWERY'	Brown body and wheels, cream logo

Tankers

November 1989	'HEYGATES FLOUR'	Brown cab, white tank brown/blue logo
November 1989	'LORD RAYLEIGH'S FARMS'	Light blue cab, darker blue chassis, white tank, blue logo
December 1989	'CENTURY OILS'	Black body, white/yellow logo
December 1989	'J & BUNN LTD'	All cream body, gold logo

Commissioned Models expected late 1989 early 1990
i) 'SHELL MEX' 'BP'   ii) MANSFIELD BREWERY (Stretton Models)

A.E.C. Regent — Double Decker Bus

December 1989	'BIRDS EYE'	No further details available
December 1989	'SCHWEPPES'	No further details available

Packaging
Models are housed in white/grey window boxes with the models well packed within a plastic mould cover

Price & Rarity Gradings
This will be provided in the next edition of the Catalogue which is due to be published in October 1990 by which time market price levels should have become established.

Crescent Toys

Quality mint boxed models or indeed lower grade boxed models extremely difficult to find. Consequently with so few models available for comparison the price ranges shown have mainly been based on models sold at auction. Again because of scarcity reasons it has not proved possible to price every model and so examples from each section have been provided.

Early Post War Models

800	Jaguar Unboxed	£25-£35	804	Police Car Unboxed	£20-£30
802/3	Locomotive Unboxed	£15-£25	425	Saloon Car Unboxed	£25-£35

Farm Equipment

1803	Dexta Tractor and Trailer	£55-£65	All Farm Wagon issues	£15-£20
1809	Dexta Tractor	£45-£55	All Trailer issues	£5-£10

Lacy Scott Auction November 1988 1809 Dextra Tractor   £50

Diecast Action Toy

1272	Scammell Scarab and Box Trailer	£65-£75	1276 Scammel Scarab & 'SHELL' Tanker	£70-£80
1274	Scammell Scarab and Low Loader	£65-£75		

Lacy Scott Auction February 1989 1274 Scammell Scarab and Low Loader £75

Military Models

Whilst our Survey recorded many mint boxed sets of field guns and howitzers no large military vehicles were seen, any information collectors can provide on the prices of these models would be welcomed.

Prices for armoured cars	£15-£25	Prices for Gun Models	£10-£15

Historical Models

1913 Coronation Stage Coach boxed	£45-£55	Later coach issues	£10-£15
145 Medieval Catapult	£10-£15		

Miniature Wild West

No price details available — again any information on the details of models or prices would be welcomed.

Grand Prix Racing Cars

Most boxed model all issues   £65-£75

Long Vehicles & Trukkers

No price or model details available

Spot On Models

Since the 1988 Market Survey the market for Spot On Models has tended to slow down somewhat. Consequently the prices listed do not require amendment at this time. As can be seen from Auction Price Results the demand for Spot On has been steady if not spectacular. Prices therefore have levelled out and this position is hardly surprising where one considers how quickly Spot On prices have risen over the last few years.

Auction Price Results
*Phillips West Two London 1989 Auction &
Lacy Scott's , Bury St. Edmunds 1989*

117	Jones Crane (G-E) boxed	£90
207	Wadhams Ambulance (E) boxed	£140
106 A/oc	Austin Prime Mover (E) blue with MG 'A' in crate	£200
111A	Ford Thames Trader with Log Load (G-E)	£120
110/ 2b	A.E.C. Mammoth 'LONDON BRICK' with lead boxed (G-E)	£120
101	Armstrong Siddeley (M) boxed	£85
213	Ford Anglia (M) boxed	£65
217	'E' type Jaguar (M) unboxed	£65
114	Jaguar 3-4 (M) box damaged	£50
271	Express Dairy Van (M) box damaged	£60
120	Fiat Multipla (M) boxed	£50
106/A1	Austin Prime Mover (M) boxed	£160
417	Bedford Army KItchen (M) boxed	£40
801	At home with Tommy Spot (M) boxed	£85
217 2A	'SHELL' garage set	£30

Catalogue Amendment
New Entry

265	1964 'TONIBELL DAIRY ICE CREAM' Van New Zealand issue Turquoise body	£125-£150

Cover Picture
This depicts the Spot On Routemaster Bus and the Spot On Royal Rolls Royce.

Tri-Ang Minic Ships

This is a relatively small sector of the market place and the only price changes noted have effected the lower priced models

M701	RMS Caronia	£35-£40	M721	HMS Britannia	£20-£25
702	RMS Queen Elizaeth	£35-£40	M712H	HMS Britannia	£10-£15
M703	RMS Queen Mary	£25-£30	M728	Britannia Queen	£15-£20
M704	S.S. United States	£25-£30	M729	Bristol Queen	£15-£20
M705	S.S. Nieuw Amsterdam	£40-£50	M730	Cardiff Queen	£15-£20
M708	Saxonia	£25-£30	M732	S.S. Varicella	£25-£35
M709	Ivernia	£25-£30			
M710	RMS Sylvania	£25-£30		Gift Sets & Presentation Pack	
M711	Carinthia	£25-£30		No Price changes recorded	

Lledo — 'Models of Days Gone'
Review of Listings

DG 001 Horse Drawn Tram

| 001 | Amend listing to show prices of i) ii) & iii) as | £10-£15 |

DG 006 Model 'T' Ford Van

004	'BRITISH MEAT'	
	'DG6 — DG' baseplate	£20-£25
	'DG6 — DG 8'	£5-£8
048	'HARDWARE JOURNAL'	£20-£25
053	'CANADA CRAFT & HOBBY'	£60-£65
054	'CANADA TRAVEL'	£60-£65
056	'TOYFAIR' issues 1986/7/8/9	£10-£15
	1986 'W' HARROWGATE variant	£40-£50

DG 009 Model 'A' Ford Open Car

| 001 | 'POLICE' Car two tone blue | £10-£15 |

DG 010 1934 Albion Single Deck Bus

| 005 | 'SOUTHERN VECTIS' white logo one side | £15-£20 |

DG 012 1934 Fire Engine

| 011 | First issue Boston Fire Engine | £10-£15 |

DG 013 1929 Ford Model 'A' Van

| 017 | 'MITRE 10' (Special Box) | £15-£20 |
| 021 | 'F.D.B.' (Danish Co-op) | £20-£25 |

DG 015 1932 Regent Double Decker

001	'HALL'S WINE' smooth roof variant	£45-£55
	'HALL'S WINE' tan version	£15-£20
	'HALL'S WINE' silver roof/brass radiator version has been re-released delete £45	NRP

DG 019
1932 A.E.C. Regal Single Deck Coach

| 001 | 'SOUTHEND' blue with filler cap | £40-£50 |
| | Red with filler cap | £50-£60 |

DG 018 1937 Packard Enclosed Van

| 006 | 'CAMPERDOWN' | £35-£40 |
| | 'ST. MARY'S HOSPITAL' (3000 certificates) | £12-£15 |

DG 019 Rolls Royce Phantom II

| 002 | All cream body | £25-£35 |

DG 031 Horse Drawn Brewery Dray

| 002 | 'EVERARDS' | £10-£12 |

Lledo — 'Models of Days Gone' — New Issues

DG 001 Horse Drawn Tram

No additional issues

DG 002 Horse Drawn Milk Float

No additional issues

DG 003 Horse Drawn Delivery Van

| 013 | 1988 'J. SPRATT' |

DG 004 Horse Drawn Omnibus

Add 'RADIO TIMES' existing listing reference nos i) 010, ii) 011, iii) 012

| 012 | 1989 'COLMANS MUSTARD' |

DG 005 Horse Drawn Fire Engine

| 009 | 1989 'CARROW ROAD' (Colmans) |

DG 006 1920 Model 'T' Ford Van

| 062 | 'TOYFAIR 88' (Trade only) |
| 063 | 'LLEDO WORLDWIDE CC' |

064	'CHARRINGTON'
065	'HAMLEYS' (88 logo)
066	'BUDWEISER'
067	'GOLDEN SHRED'
068	'MILLBANK/SCHIFFER'
069	-081 Canadian Provinces Models
082	'THE WINCHESTER CLUB'
083	'WALLS ICE CREAM'
084	'TRADE FAIR 89' (Trade only)
085	'SCNEIDERS' (German)
086	'AU BON MARCHE' (France)
087	'SELFRIDGES'
088	'YORKSHIRE MOORS RAILWAY'
089	'BRITANNIA FILMS' gold plated
090	'HIS MASTERS VOICE'
091	'SHELL'

N.B Plastic bases introduced in 1988

DG 007
1934 Model 'A' Ford 'WOODY WAGON'

| 009 | 1988 'CASTROL OIL' |
| 010 | 1988 'FORD SALES & SERVICE' |

DG 008 1920 Model 'T' Ford Tanker

Add the following reference numbers to the existing listing

012	'HOMEPRIDE' and 013 — 'SHELL'
014	1988 'DUCKHAMS'
015	1989 'SHELL FRANCE'
016	1989 'BP'
013	1988 'J. SPRATT'
	1989 'TEXACO'

All models have 'C' type barplates — DG6-8

DG 009 1934 Model 'A' Ford Car

No New Issues

DG 010 1933 Albion Single Decker Bus

Amend the existing listing to read as follows
016 'OAKRIDGE SCHOOL BUS' & 017 'SILVER SERVICE'. Delete 'BILLINGSGATE'

018	1988 'E.B. TAYLOR'
019	1989 'COVENTRY'

DG 011 Horse Drawn Large Van

009	1988 'BUDWEISER'
010	1988 'SMITHFIELDS MARKET'
013	1989 'BROWNS OF BELFAST'

DG 012 1934 Fire Engine

010	1988 'GLASGOW'
011	1988 'BOSTON'
012	1989 'BIRMINGHAM'

DG 013 1919 Model 'A' Ford Vans

025	'EXCHANGE & MART'
026	'EVER READY'
027	'HEINZ TOMATO SOUP'
028	1988 'CHARLES TATE'
029	1988 'ELIZABETH SHAW'
030	1989 'EMPIRE'
031	1989 'AQUASCUTUM'
032	1989 'BBC 50TH ANNIVERSARY'
033	1989 'KLEENEX'
034	1989 'ALLENBURYS DIET'
—	1989 'OXYDOL'

Type C baseplates DG 7-9-13-14

DG 014 1930 Model 'A' Ford Car

No additional issues

DG 015
1932 A.E.C. Regent Double Decker Bus

018	1988 'LLEDO COLLECTORS CLUB'
019	1989 'TERRY'S MOBILE GYM'
021	1989 'MAPLES PIANOS'
021	1989 'ST. IVEL CHEESE'

DG 016
1934 Dennis Heavy Goods Vehicle

016	1988 'ABELS'
017	1988 'HAMLEYS' (88 logo)
018	1989 'ALLIED REMOVERS'
019	1989 'COSMOS LAMPS'
020	1989 'GOODYEAR TYRES'

DG 017
1932 A.E.C. Regal Single Deck Coach

014	1988 'HAMLEYS' (88 logo)
015	1988 'SUTTONS'
016	1988 'ROYAL NAVY'
017	1989 'ROYAL BLUE'
018	1989 'YORKSHIRE MOORS RAILWAY'
019	1989 'COLCHESTER CORPORATION'

DG 018   1937 Packard Enclosed Van

010	1988 'NATIONAL WESTMINISTER'
011	1988 'FOTORAMA'
012	1988 'PERRONI'
013	1988 'ST. MARY'S HOSPITAL'
014	1989 'LEYLAND PAINTS'

Type B baseplates

DG 019
1931 Rolls Royce Phantom II (Brewster)

006	1989 Ruby Wedding issue
007	1988 Charcoal body
008	1988 MINDERS — gold body
009	1988 'WORLDWIDE CLUB' silver body
010	1989 Green body with coachlines

DG 020   1936 Ford Stake Truck

008	1988 'IND COOPE'
009	1988 'BUDWEISER'
010	1988 'H.M.S. ROOKE'
011	1988 'WATNEYS'
012	1989 'CALORGAS'

DG 021   1934 Chevrolet Van

005	1988	'LLEDO WORLDWIDE'
006	1988	'DR PEPPER'
007	1988	'HAMLEYS' (88 logo)
008	1988	'BIRDS CUSTARD'
009	1988	'BUDWEISER'
010	1988	'FARRAH'S TOFFERS'
011	1988	'VITA WHEAT'
012	1989	'HERSHEY'S KISSES'
013	1989	'MAJESTIC FILMS'
014	1989	'SIMPSON'S'
015	1989	'CHERRY BLOSSOM'
014	1988	'HAMLEYS' (88 logo)

DG 022   1933 Town Deliver Van

006	1988	'HAMLEYS' (88 logo)
007	1988	'PIZZA EXPRESS'
008	1988	'BUDWEISER'
009	1988	'TESCO'S'
010	1989	'SOHO DAIRY'
014	1988	'HAMLEYS' (88 logo)

DG 023   1954 Scenicruiser

No additional issues

DG 024   1934 Rolls Royce Playboy

003	1987	Red/white body
004	1987	Silver lustre (Charcoal) body
005	1988	Bright green/black body
006	1989	Dark green/black with coachlines

N.B. All other details as per existing listings

DG 025
1925 Rolls Royce Silver Ghost (Barker)

002	1987	Silver body/blue body
003	1987	White/black body
004	1988	Metallic grey/black
005	1989	Dark green/black with coachlines

DG 026   1934 Chevrolet Drinks Wagon

006	1988	'BUDWEISER'
007	1988	'CORONA DRINKS'
008	1989	'CANADA DRY'
014	1988	'HAMLEYS' (88 logo)
		i) Unreadable near logo
		ii) Readable near logo

DG 027   1938 Mack Breakdown Truck

003	1989	'MOBILOIL'
004	1989	'ARTHUR DALEY'
005	1989	'MOBILOIL' (France)
014	1988	'HAMLEYS' (88 logo)

DG 028
1937 Mack 'Canvas Back' Truck

002	1988	'HEINZ BAKED BEANS'
003	1988	'LLEDO WORLDWIDE'
004	1988	'TATE & LYLE'S'
005	1988	'FIELD GUN CREW' RN
006	1989	'DUNLOP TYRES'
007	1989	'YORKSHIRE MOORS RAILWAY'

DG 029   1942 Dodge 4 x 4

001	1989	U.S. Field Ambulance
014	1988	'HAMLEYS' (88 logo)
	1989	R.A.F. AIRCREW

DG 030   1939 Chevy Panel Van

001	1989	'JOHN BULL TYRES'
002	1989	'FRY'S CHOCOLATE'
003	1989	'LIPTONS TEA'

DG 031   Horse Drawn Brewers Dray

001	1988	'WHITBREAD'
002	1988	'EVERARD'S'
003	1989	'TRUMAN'
004	1989	'GREENE KING'
014	1988	'HAMLEYS' (88 logo)

DG 032   1907 Rolls Royce Silver Ghost

001	1988	All silver body, maroon seats
002	1989	Dark green/cream with Coachlines

DG 033   1920 Model 'T' Ford Car

001	1989	Black body red seats
002	1989	'SINGER SEWING MACHINE'

DG 034   Dennis Delivery Van

001	1989	'SMEDLEYS' Dark green/black
002	1989	'HOVIS FOR TEA' All dark cream

DG 035   Dennis Fire Service Limousine

001   1989 'EDINBURGH'

DG 036   1939 Chevy Pick-Up

001   1989 'BUCK & HICKMAN' Dark Green

DG 037   1932 Ford Model 'A' Panel Van

001   1989   'CANADIAN   CLUB WHISKY' Brown/black body

DG 038
1925 Rolls Royce Silver Ghost Saloon

001   1989 Dark Green/cream with coachlines

DG 039   1934 Mack Truck

1989 'TARMAC CRANE TRUCK'
1989 'NATIONAL BENZOLE'
1989 'GAS LIGHT & COKE CO'

Collector Packs & Limited Sets

1988 Royal Navy Set DG 017, DG 024 and DG 025

1989 The Gold Plated Quartet — British Film Company Models
Hand finished 24 Carat gold-plated set of film models:-

DG 006 'BRITANNIA FILMS', DG 018 'B & C FILMS'
DG 013 'EMPIRE FILMS', DG 021 'MAJESTIC FILMS'
10000 issued — UK Price £40.00

1989 Famous Stores of London Set

Four Models depicting well known stores

DG 006 — 089 'SELFRIDGES',

DG013-033 'AQUASCUTUM' DG018-016 'FORTNUM & MASONS'   DG 013 'SIMPSONS'

DG 006 1920 Model 'T' Ford Van — Canadian Provinces Set
A set of twelve models issued in 1988. Logos as follows:
069—'ALBERTA', 070—'BRITISH COLUMBIA', 071—'CANADA',   072—'MANITOBA',   073—'NEW BRUSWICK',   074—'NEWFOUNDLAND',   075—'NORTH WEST TERRITORIES', 076—'NOVA SCOTIA', 077—'ONTARIO', 078—'PRINCE EDWARD ISLAND', 079—'QUEBEC', 080—'SASKATCHEWAN', 081—'YUKON'
1,000 sets issued UK price £35-£45

Lledo Promotionals

LP006	'FARNHAM MALTINGS'	£20-£25	LP016	'SURREY DIECAST CLUB' (500)	£15-£20
LP013	'BUCKTROUT'	£5-£7	LP016	'AVON DIECAST CLUB' (500)	£15-£20
LP013	'VECTIS MODELS'	£10-£15	LP016	'AVON ROAD RESCUE (?)'	£75-£100
LP015	'CITY OF LONDON' (500) with certificate	£65-£75	LP016	'OVERDRIVE MANPOWER' Special Box	£75-£100
LP015	'ADMIRALS CUP' (500)	£40-£50			

Grey Series (New Entry)

Models produced in 1986 as samples for possible North American 'Promotional' customers. They have a neutral colour of grey and carry no designs whatsoever but are advertised for sale usually for £10-£15 each

Odds and Ends

3rd Edition British Diecast Model Toys Catalogue

A further supply has now become available and may be obtained from your usual shop/dealer or if in difficulty send to:-

Swapmeet Toys & Models Ltd, PO Box 21, Bury St., Edmunds, Suffolk, England, IP33 2ED. Terms UK £9.95 per copy (includes postage). Overseas orders. Payment by Sterling Draft. Postage and Packing please enclose: Europe Surface £3. Air Mail £4; USA Surface £3.50, Air Mail £11; Australia Surface £3.75; Air Mail £11.50

Trade Terms

Please contact us for details of the excellent trade terms available both for the main 3rd Edition Catalogue and for this Supplement.

Advertising Amendment to the 3rd Edition

Please note that the half page advertisement at the bottom of page 24 is 'DAVID HINAM'S', Specialist Mail Order dealer of 278 Ashgate Road, Chesterfield S40 4AW Tel: (0246 232832)

New Books

Title:- **Collecting Matchbox Diecast Toys —**
The First Forty Years Price £34.95
Highly recommended — an absolute must for the serious collector. Available from Matchbox appointed stockists or MICA, 42 Bridge St. Row, Chester CH1 1NQ.

Title:- **The Great Book of Corgi 1956-83**
Limited Edition Price £49.99 includes a special edition Routemaster Bus.
A unique history of every model produced containing 1000 illustrations and 700 colour plates. Available from Corgi Collector Culb, Corgi Toys Ltd., Kingsway, Swansea Industrial Estate, Swansea, SA5 4EL.

N.B. See Corgi Routemaster Bus Section for details of special bus issue with this publication.

New Abbreviations

AHC	Authentic Hub Caps	MLCD	Multicoloured
AG	Authentic Grille	MNP	Metal Number Plate
AW	Authentic Wheels	MOM	Mail Order Model
BGPW	Black or Grey Plastic Wheels	NE	New Entry
CHL	Chrome Headlight Lenses	PHL	Plastic Headlights
DHD	Detachable Hood	PLI	Plastic Interior
DFS	Drivers Foot Step	PNP	Plastic Number Plates
DTR	Detailed Transmission	RFB	Roof Beacon
GBT	Globetrotter	RRT	Removable Rubber Tyres
GSM	Gift Set Model	SBHW	Solid Bolt Head Wheels
IBL	Indicators and Brake Lights	SPC	Supercedes
LHD	Left Hand Drive	SPLT	Spotlights
MIC	Made in China	TLC	Translucent finish
MIM	Made in Macau		

Auction Price Result Abbreviations:-

(M)	Mint	(E-M)	Excellent to Mint
(G-E)	Good to Excellent		

Advertising in the 4th Edition

The 4th Edition is due to be published on the 31st October 1990 and because of its unique position on thousands of collectors bookshelves the Catalogue offers the ideal opportunity for good value long term advertising.

TYPES OF ADVERTISING BEST SUITED TO THE CATALOGUE
— Model Shop Addresses and Services
— Mail Order Services
— Auction House Services and Dates
— Long Term Toyfair Dates
— Wholesale Services to the trade
— General Advertising etc.

Several traders both large and small took up the opporunity to advertise in the 3rd edition and have been delighted with the response from the thousands of users of the Catalogue. Now therefore is your chance to share in the success of the 4th Edition by booking space in the catalogue.

Simply complete and return the advertising enquiry section and we shall be pleased to send you details of our terms and conditions.

N.B. The last date that we shall be able to receive copy will be April 30th 1990

To Swapmeet Toys & Models Ltd.
PO Box 21, Bury St. Edmunds, Suffolk IP33 2ED

I/we are interested in advertising in the 4th Edition of the British Diecast Model Toys Catalogue. Please send me/us completely without any obligation, full details of your advertising terms and conditions.

Name ....

Address ....

....